THE BOOK OF THE LION

A SOMALI LION KILLED BY SIR A. E. PEASE.

Mounted by E. Gerrard, Camden Town. Photographed by Dickenson.

THE BOOK OF
THE LION

Sir Alfred E. Pease

Peter Capstick, Series Editor

St. Martin's Press
New York

To the Reader:

The editors and publishers of the Peter Capstick Adventure Library faced significant responsibilities in the faithful reprinting of Africa's great hunting books of long ago. Essentially, they saw the need for each text to reflect to the letter the original work, nothing having been added or expunged, if it was to give the reader an authentic view of another age and another world.

In deciding that historical veracity and honesty were the first considerations, they realized that it meant retaining many distasteful racial and ethnic terms to be found in these old classics. The firm of St. Martin's Press, Inc., therefore wishes to make it very clear that it disassociates itself and its employees from the abhorrent racial-ethnic attitudes of the past which may be found in these books.

History is the often unpleasant record of the way things actually were, not the way they should have been. Despite the fact that we have no sympathy with the prejudices of decades past, we feel it better—and indeed, our collective responsibility—not to change the unfortunate facts that were.

—Peter Hathaway Capstick

Library of Congress Cataloging-in-Publication Data

Pease, Alfred E. (Alfred Edward), Sir, 1857–1939.
   The book of the lion.

   1. Lion hunting.   2. Lions.   I. Title.
SK305.L5P4   1986   798.2′774428   86-26196
ISBN 0-312-00108-8

Editor's Note
to the Reprint Edition

January 29, 1911 [Kenya, British East Africa Protectorate]:

Before relating what happened in the afternoon of the fatal day, I may explain that it was our practice when we had a novice or someone new to "the game" as we played it, to take care that in every dangerous situation our guests, whether they were aware of it or not, had an experienced and deadly shot standing by.

For this purpose no more reliable men could be found than the Hill cousins and our sole object this day was to see that George Grey killed a lion . . . and that Howard Pease should get his first shot at one.

The speaker, Sir Alfred Edward Pease, a Yorkshireman by birth and second baronet of Hutton Low Cross and Pinchinthorpe, was leader and host of the party that day on his estate on the Athi Plains. He and Clifford Hill decided to move off toward Potha, a hill where his great friend and neighbor, the venerated Philip Percival, was to build his house. Sir Alfred and Hill had indeed found two large and well-maned lions—which they tried to drive toward Wami Hill nearby—but the other members of the party had pushed on too quickly and were fouling up the effort.

The newcomers were spoiling our game, for the lions now turned straight up Wami. I yelled and waved but only one of the party paid attention to my frantic efforts. Another, to my horror, I saw was gaining rapidly on the rear lion. Still I never dreamed he was going to ride it down. . . . Hill yelled, "Shoot! . . . . Shoot! . . . Shoot him!" I was off my horse and shouted "Too far—300 yards." Hill yelled "No—200!" and fired. I saw his bullet strike up dust ten feet short of the rear lion which had whipped around and started his charge. The charge started before I got my rifle to my shoulder . . . then it was over. I saw every detail. As the lion charged, Grey leapt from his pony and received the charge in perfect style; fired on the instant at 25 yards; again at 5 yards, as quick as is possible with a magazine-rifle in the hand of an expert.

These 3 or 4 seconds were ones of agonizing suspense. Is the lion going to drop? Ping! . . . The lion flying straight on. . . . Ping! again; and Grey hurled to the ground, shaken like a rat by a terrier, and I was galloping, as hard as I could to the scene. Only a few hundred yards seemed like a mile. I was conscious that my son [Howard Pease] was doing the same thing and by the time he and I were on our feet by the lion, Hill was there too.

As we arrived, the lion stopped worrying Grey for a second and glared at us. Grey was underneath. The other lion crouched in the grass close to, grunting and lashing his tail. The first lion then got hold of Grey [again] and he could only fire into the lion's body, and even that was risky. We all fired. Hill's .450-bullet in the lungs practically knocked the lion out, and allowed me to put the muzzle of my rifle to his head and finish him. Hill then shouted that his rifle had jammed and urged me to shoot the other lion. I reckoned if I did not kill him dead he would get my son who was nearest, and thinking Grey was dead, I could not depend on myself to do it with a quick .256 shot. Then out of the corner of my eye I saw the big lion get up and start walking away. We pulled the first lion off Grey, and I knelt down beside him, thinking he was dead.

Grey opened his eyes and spoke very quietly to me. "I am very badly hurt. . . . I want to tell you, and you must remember I say it, that I alone am to blame for what has happened." In the same quiet way he told us how we were to move him and how to set about dressing his wounds. I had a water-bottle, and gave him a drink. His face and lips were torn down and one ear nearly off. Hill put half of my bottle of crystals of permanganate into the water-bottle, and we cut off his shirt and clothes from his mangled arms and body. In a few moments, we had washed over his face, head, arms, thighs, and body with the solution. His elbow-points were bitten right through, his hands torn to pieces, and without a syringe all we could do was to put the crystals into the deep punctures and wounds as far as we dared. Later he asked what we had done about the lion. "Have you skinned him?" "No." "Then you must skin him and take great care of the skin."

George Grey, brother of the British Foreign Secretary with the longest uninterrupted service, and founder of the Grey's Scouts at the time of the Matabele Rebellion in 1896, died of his more than sixty wounds a few days later on February 3, 1911. It was just as well. He had been dreadfully mauled and his injuries were appalling.

The Book of the Lion does not contain the foregoing information, which appears instead in Sir Alfred Pease's personal diary. The very first sentence of the Introduction to the book states that Pease had finished most of the manuscript "several years ago" but that "a great sorrow" postponed his writing. Considering that the date of publication was 1913, one wonders if the sorrow referred to was not perhaps the double tragedy of his losing his wife, Helen, after some thirty years of marriage, combined with the death of his distinguished friend, George Grey. Maybe Sir Alfred felt some sense of guilt in that latter regard, although nobody ever held him responsible, and such self-inflicted remorse would have been quite undeserved. The fact that the Grey tragedy is ignored in Pease's book, except for the briefest allusion to the type of bullet that Grey fired at the lion, does perhaps indicate that Sir Alfred must have been greatly affected by that incident.

This book is prized Africana, noted for its accuracy on lions and lion hunting, particularly for a book published so early. Sir Alfred captured the essence of lion hunting when he wrote: "He who has never been frightened by a lion must have missed half the sport of lion-hunting. Where there is no fear there can be no courage."

The book is dedicated to Theodore Roosevelt, who hunted his first lions with Sir Alfred in 1909, shortly after his term of office as President had come to an end (and not long before the death of George Grey). Those lion hunts with the Hills, Philip Percival, and Pease ushered in the era of professionally conducted safaris for clients in British East Africa.

EDITOR'S NOTE

Sir Alfred Pease was born on June 29, 1857, the heir to Sir Joseph Witwell Pease, the first Quaker baronet and president of the Peace Society. The family owned some 2,500 acres in Yorkshire, where they also had an iron and coal business. When his father died, Alfred acceded to the baronetcy in 1903; his mother, the former Mary Fox, had died in 1892.

Sir Alfred was educated at Trinity College, Cambridge, where he read for a Bachelor of Arts (Honors degree). He became a deputy lieutenant and justice of the peace, eventually serving as a member of Parliament for York City from 1885 to 1892. He also served on the City Council of North Riding where he was Alderman, thus upholding the family tradition of public service (Sir Alfred's grandfather having also been a member of Parliament).

Pease was adventurous. Between 1891 and 1912, he visited Asia Minor, Algeria, Tunisia and the Sahara, Somaliland, Abyssinia, Kenya, and Uganda, hunting wherever he could. He was Resident Magistrate of the Transvaal in Komatipoort, next to present-day Mozambique, from 1903 to 1905, and he worked in the Allied Remount Service from 1914 to 1918. A keen explorer and hunter, Sir Alfred also sketched. He went on to write thirteen books embracing subjects as varied as wildlife, a dictionary on the North Riding dialect, and oases in Algeria!

In 1907, Sir Alfred went to Kenya where he

gradually settled and became firm friends with
the renowned lion hunters Clifford and Harold
Hill, who were neighbors. Another neighbor and
eventual partner in an ostrich farming venture
was Philip Percival, who was to become the
Shogun of the East African Professional Hunters
Association and one of the truly great names in
African hunting. Pease honed his hunting skills
in such company and then shot to international
prominence in 1908, during a visit to America,
where he met the then President, Theodore
Roosevelt, and promptly invited him to come out
to Kenya and hunt from his "hunting lodge."

To what must have been Pease's absolute horror, the President accepted the offer as bully.
The only problem was that Pease did not *have* a
hunting lodge! He was hard pressed to build one
of stone before the former President's arrival in
1909 with a large retinue of reporters and aides
and his famed pigskin library. This lodge, overlooking the Athi Plains, was to become Percival's
home.

On this expedition, Roosevelt's first two lions
were no bigger than "mastiffs," which was unlikely to have overly pleased the ex-President, although he did take a couple of good ones with
Pease and his neighbors, the Hills and Philip
Percival. Despite Roosevelt's laudatory letter to
Sir Alfred at the beginning of *The Book of The
Lion,* there is a suspicion that the two men did
not get along all that well. This is based on the

fact that Pease is rather obviously omitted from the acknowledgments in Roosevelt's *African Game Trails*, although Pease had been his host for two weeks and had gone to no end of trouble for his distinguished guest.

This suspicion is further strengthened by what Roosevelt's grandson, Kermit, wrote in his book *Sentimental Safari* (Knopf, 1963, New York).

There are many stories about the adventures of the people whom TR encountered on the trip, and thumbnail sketches of individuals such as Philip Percival and the Hill cousins, who made such a deep impression on TR. But his host on his arrival, Sir Alfred Pease, and his host subsequently at Juju Farm and later in Nairobi, Mr. McMillan, and the hunters, Cunninghame, Tarlton and Quentin Grogan are not really portrayed at all.

Sir Alfred's first wife gave him two sons and a daughter, one son dying in the First World War. He remarried in 1912, the same year in which he decided to sell his Kenya estate and return to England. A widower once more in 1922, Pease remarried during the same year and had a fresh family of two sons and a daughter, the elder son later becoming Sir (Alfred) Vincent Pease, fourth baronet. The Dowager Lady Pease died in 1979, a solid 122 years after her husband's birth! Financial misfortune seems to have struck later on in Sir Alfred's life when he wrote to his great friend, Denis Lyell, the hunter, naturalist, and author, in 1924 saying: "I am afraid I have read very few books on sport and travel—the fact is I am now 'a stay at home' man, and in these days I cannot afford to buy books and only read the reviews of them in the papers."

The Book of the Lion remains the earliest completely authentic and enrapturing account on the subject of lions, especially from the hunter's point of view. It was none other than Denis Lyell who said that this book was ". . . one of the best accounts of his and others' experiences with these animals which has ever been published." Leslie Tarlton wrote in 1926 that ". . . The days when Pease, Cunninghame, Delamere, and so forth galloped lions and shot them with a small bore are the only days that count in my estimation. . . ."

Sir Alfred was spared the Second World War, dying on April 27, 1939, after a long, varied, and unusual life. There is an added poignancy to Pease's words, read as they are decades later against the background of a vastly altered world, especially concerning African hunting:

The generation to which I belong has seen Africa yield up her secrets; and the survivors of this generation, who have witnessed the passing away or transformation of many of the great game regions, alone can tell of what our generation has done and seen, and which

EDITOR'S NOTE

those who come after can never do or see
again.

—PETER HATHAWAY CAPSTICK

TO

THE HONOURABLE COLONEL

THEODORE ROOSEVELT

WHO, IN HIS OWN PERSON, HAS PROVED

THAT THE VERY BEST OF SPORTSMEN

MAY RENDER THE VERY BEST OF SERVICES

TO THE COMMONWEALTH OF THE WORLD

On Safari, B.E.A.,

16th October 1909.

To Sir Alfred E. Pease.

Dear Sir Alfred,—I am very much pleased that you are to write a book about lion-hunting. Very, very few people have an experience which better justifies such a book. It is the king of all sports when carried on as you have carried it on, especially when you gallop the lion, and then kill him on foot as he charges or prepares to charge as a lion thus rounded up will generally do. I am peculiarly pleased to have you write the book, for it was under your guidance that I first tried lion-hunting.

Sincerely yours,

THEODORE ROOSEVELT.

INTRODUCTION

ALMOST the whole of this book was written
several years ago. A great sorrow destroyed
at that time all inclination to finish it. I have
on re-reading my MS. decided to publish it,
believing that after all it may be of use as
well as of interest.

Lions and their ways have so often been
written about that almost more courage is required to take up the pen than a rifle in dealing
with them. There are very nearly as many
opinions on lions and their ways as there are
naturalists and sportsmen. I may, and indeed
hope to, arouse criticism and controversy, for
it is only by inciting other observers to relate
what they know that the truth as regards the
life history and habits of animals can be arrived
at. So that, though this book goes forth mainly
for those who have not yet met the King of
Beasts face to face in the African forest and
the wilderness, it has been written in the hope
that it may be read also by African naturalists,
sportsmen, and explorers. Incidentally I desire
that what is here set down may encourage the
British public to insist that one little corner

of our vast Empire shall remain a sanctuary for that royal creature which with our national modesty we have selected as the emblem of our own valour and magnanimity. Such a refuge now exists in the Game Reserves of the British East African Protectorate, but there are some settlers who press for the extermination of lions within the protected areas by every means, including poison and traps. None of these persons have farms or residences within the Reserves. The Southern Game Reserve (of B.E.A.) is unsuitable for settlement on account of the climate and the want of water, even were the available and suitable areas exhausted, an event which is remote. Few of those who complain of lions moving out of the Reserves into the settled parts have resided and farmed as near to the boundaries of the sanctuary as the writer, and none he knows of have had more to do in repelling occasional sorties and in defending their live stock. There are millions of acres where noisy agitators such as these can settle in tame security. The few who clamour to be allowed to make short work of all the game for the sake of a passing profit in hides would be the loudest in their lamentations when all the game and all their sport had gone for ever. Those who have settled in such places knew the conditions and in many cases selected a game district deliberately, the very presence of game and wild beasts being an added, if not the chief, attraction. Sated themselves with excitement, they would deprive posterity of the pleasure they once had in the presence of the game.

As regards African game in general, as distinct from the carnivora and beasts of prey, it must be remembered that extermination does not necessarily come about by the actual slaughter of a particular species. Mere disturbance or epidemic diseases may reduce the numbers of any sort of game to a point where indiscriminate shooting will complete very quickly its disappearance.

The author has talked to an old Vortrekker in the Orange River Colony who was one of the first to enter the country. The old Dutchman stretched out his hand over the lifeless plains and mountains, and said: " When I first came here the whole of this was covered with countless herds of game, of giraffe and of quagga; you could never believe that it could vanish in the lifetime of a man, but nothing remains ! "

He lamented the disappearance of the vast herds that roamed over the veldt, and indignantly denied that their extermination was due to the shooting and hide-hunting. He declared that quagga, hartebeest, wildebeest, and buck were present in such countless thousands that had all the settlers in the country shot ceaselessly throughout their lives they could not have wiped them out. This from my experience in other parts of Africa I believe to be true to this extent, namely, that it was not actual *killing* that in the beginning thinned their numbers seriously, but disturbance and hunting which caused the great herds to migrate to regions less suitable, or altogether unsuitable, for their existence— districts where food, water, climate, and other circumstances were against them and their young. Yet undoubtedly, as the game diminished and was driven farther afield, it was finally killed out by the meat and hide hunters. When any species becomes rare, it is the more sought after by trophy hunters, and the settler gave the old excuse that if he did not shoot, his neighbours would.

Many wild animals require vast space where they can follow the rains for the grass that springs up where thunderstorms have passed. Their condition depends on access to particular herbage, feeding-grounds, and rivers at certain seasons. When they can no longer visit these in peace and security they migrate elsewhere, and if compelled to revisit the old pastures and former haunts they return in ever-diminishing numbers. In South Africa as the game fled before the settlers the hunter and trekking Boer followed, driving it into countries less and less adapted to its nature. It is a melancholy story, and it is for Englishmen to prevent its repetition. It may be stated as an established principle, requiring no new proof, that for the preservation of African fauna very extensive Reserves are necessary, and absolute freedom from molestation must be guaranteed to make protection really effective. There are some of the commonest kinds of African game which disappear quickly without much disturbance. The wildebeest will stand very little settlement in his neighbourhood and very little hunting. In a period of five years in British East Africa I have seen the wildebeest on the Kapiti Plains diminish from thousands to hundreds and from hundreds to twos and threes— yet I do not think twenty-five wildebeest were killed by settlers or hunters during these years in my immediate neighbourhood. My explanation of their rapid diminution is this. The grass remains green on the foot-hills round the Mua and Lukania mountains long after the plains are dried up. These pastures carried the game through the annual periods of drought and preserved it in abnormally rainless years. I have seen a large proportion of the vast herds of the Athi and Kapiti Plains at such times gathered together on this ground in such enormous masses that it is impossible to give any idea of their numbers. But this is the very ground that has been taken up by settlers, and though the colonists are not very numerous their presence is enough to scare away so wild and timid a species as the wildebeest. During the same period there was no very marked diminution in the herds of zebra, impala, kongoni

(Coke's hartebeest), Grant's gazelle, Thomson's gazelle, and other game, which is much less sensitive to man's presence. All these latter species might in these dry seasons be seen feeding right up to the houses of the settlers and practically with the cattle and tame ostriches. I never saw eland killed on or round my farm and never shot at one myself, but they too have gone from that part. I have always protested against the attempted extermination of any species of either big or small game.

Some years ago in a certain district of the Sudan an official urged me to kill all the hippopotami I could. I ventured to dispute the wisdom of this policy of extermination, for there were no longer such numbers of hippo that they could do very extensive damage to the native crops, and before the advent of " civilized " rule the natives had been accustomed to great numbers of them and had to exert themselves to protect their crops. Never in the history of the country have the natives suffered so little from the depredations of hippo, nor lived in such security for themselves, their lands, and their markets. To destroy utterly every creature that does a little damage to man or calls out his energy in self-defence is a revolting policy, calculated to make the world a dull place and man a dull beast. The Nilotic native is all the better for having to struggle a little with the hippos, and could the reader watch him fighting the river-horse he would be quite sure the native enjoyed the sport. No one can blame an official for carrying out the home conception of civilization, and that idea seems to be to transform the natives of the Sudan into a squalid, mud-hoeing population similar to the Delta fellaheen. This kind of progress we have realized in certain spots of our own land, and having achieved it we stand horrified and bewildered at the spectacle. Western civilization raises monsters that neither human strength nor wit can overcome, whose depredations are a thousand-fold more terrible than those of the river-horse on the banks of the White Nile.

In Game Reserves of limited extent and in protected areas where the stock of game is limited there is some excuse, and perhaps at times a necessity, in reducing lions and beasts of prey as much as possible.

In the Transvaal such a policy can be defended, for beasts of prey would otherwise have rendered it almost hopeless to attempt to save some of the most interesting species of big game and antelopes from extinction. Owing to various causes, including rinderpest and the unscrupulous destruction of big game in the Reserves and on private farms[1] in the Transvaal during the South African War, the number of giraffe, buffalo, roan, sable, kudu, eland, and other

---

[1] An African "farm" may be, and often is, an estate extending to 20,000 acres and upwards.

species were so depleted by 1903 that it would be no exaggeration to say of some of them that the survivors could be counted on the fingers of one hand. Since that date, under the wise, constant, and watchful care of Major J. Stevenson-Hamilton,[1] the Game Warden, these species have not only been saved from extinction but have increased surprisingly. He has waged continuous war on lions and vermin. His record of carnivora destroyed is not complete from the earlier portion of the period 1903 to 1908, but during this period he with his assistants accounted for (in the Transvaal Eastern Game Reserve) 70 lions, 85 leopards, 29 cheetahs, 118 spotted hyænas (*crocuta*), 4 brown hyænas (*brunea*), and 151 wild dogs (*Lycaon pictus*).

In British East Africa there exists a vast region unsuited for colonization where the game and wild animals have been protected and remain in their original condition. All lovers of wild life and all haters of extermination should support the policy of retaining it as a natural sanctuary.

[1] *Vide* Major J. Stevenson-Hamilton's Notes, p. 115.

CONTENTS

		PAGE
Dedication	. . . . . .	v
Introduction	. . . . .	ix

CHAP.

I.	Lions and Lion Lands	. . . .	1
II.	About Courage	. . . . .	20
III.	Of the Courage of Lions	. . . .	35
IV.	Of Dangerous Game	. . . .	46
V.	Of Sport—Of Terror	. . . .	69
VI.	The Lion	. . . . . .	88
VII.	The Distribution of Lions—Major Stevenson-Hamilton's Notes on South African Lions and Mr. A. L. Butler's Notes on Sudan Lions—The Destructiveness of Lions	.	109
VIII.	Lion Cubs and Tame Lions	. . .	148
IX.	The Haunts of Lions	. . . .	155
X.	The Lion's Voice—The Lion's Eye	. .	166
XI.	Some Ways of Lions—Charging Lions	. .	172
XII.	In the Lion's Jaws	. . . .	185
XIII.	The Food and Drink of Lions	. .	192

CHAP. PAGE

XIV. LION-HUNTING—TRACKING LIONS . . . 200

XV. HUNTING LIONS WITH DOGS — HUNTING LIONS
ON HORSEBACK 238

XVI. NIGHT-SHOOTING—LASSOING LIONS. . . 246

XVII. A FEW HINTS FOR BEGINNERS . . . 254

APPENDIX I. THE LION IN ANCIENT HISTORY . 259

APPENDIX II. RIFLES AND PROJECTILES FOR DAN-
GEROUS GAME . . 267

APPENDIX III. SOME NAMES FOR THE LION IN
AFRICA . . . 281

APPENDIX IV. ADDENDUM TO CHAPTER VII., re
LIONS IN BRITISH EAST
AFRICA . . . 283

INDEX 287

LIST OF ILLUSTRATIONS

A SOMALI LION ON A ZEBRA . . . *Frontispiece*

FACING PAGE

THE QUAGGA (NOW EXTINCT) 24

A LION CHARGE 40

COLONEL ROOSEVELT KILLING HIS FIRST LION . . 96

AN ALGERIAN LION 112

SOUTH AFRICAN LIONS 140

A SACRED LION ON DONKEY-BACK 150

EXORCIZING A CAMEL 154

DEFENDING AN OSTRICH BOMA 160

LION ROARING AT DAWN 168

A CHARGING LION 176

LIONS LET OUT OF CAGE 262

ASSUR-BANI-PAL ON HORSEBACK SPEARING LION . . 262

THE "KNOCK-OUT TARGET" PRESENTED BY A LION AT, SAY, SIXTY YARDS 268

DIAGRAM TO SHOW HOW MUCH OF A LION'S BROADSIDE PRESENTS A "KNOCK-OUT TARGET" . . . 268

PAGE

SKETCH MAP SHOWING THE DISTRIBUTION OF LIONS . 109

KING HUNTING LIONS 261

WOUNDED LIONESS 262

LION SEIZING CHARIOT WHEEL 263

DIAGRAMS (APPENDIX II.): BEHAVIOUR OF BULLETS, ETC.

273 *et seq.*

THE BOOK OF THE LION

CHAPTER I

LIONS AND LION LANDS

In the years now gone I have wandered and resided in many parts of Africa—North, East, Equatorial, and South. It has been my good fortune to know many of the most experienced hunters and the best informed travellers and explorers. From my youth up I have loved travellers' tales ; the words may be a synonym for mendacities, yet with age I have become more rather than less credulous by reason of what my own eyes have seen, my own ears have heard, and my own hands have handled.

Among the men most familiar with Nature's haunts are many who never write, some scarcely talk, of their experiences or of the wonders they have seen. There have been, and are, numbers of explorers, hunters, prospectors, adventurers, and pioneers whose names you have never heard, who have seen and done far more than we who write and talk about these things. But the result of their experience is lost, and such knowledge as posterity will possess will be due to those travellers and observers who have taken the trouble to record what they have seen. The generation to which I belong has seen Africa yield up her secrets; and the survivors of this generation, who have witnessed the passing away or transformation of many of the great game regions, alone can tell of what our generation has done and seen, and which those who come after can never do or see again. Often the best writers, or at least those who are regarded by the reading public as the most instructed and authoritative on African animal life, are those who have had little or very limited experience of life in Africa. A large proportion of such authors are fond of generalizations, and some are very dogmatic in their assertions as regards the habits and ways of lions. One of my objects in giving the results of my own experience is to show that, in spite of what accepted authorities may state, lions do not *always* do this, and *never* do that. It will be my own fault if I cannot give a rational account of them and their conduct, in spite of the fact that the experiences of individual hunters must differ very considerably, and the conclusions that any one of them may come to, even from a large and varied experience, may be at fault.

Now amongst the good sportsmen I have met I have found some who considered the sport of hunting lions too dangerous to be justifiable; others who held that there was little or no

danger in their pursuit, and that the sport
required neither courage nor skill; others, and
by no means the least experienced of travellers
and hunters, who, though intensely keen to add
lions to their trophies, have failed always and
everywhere to meet them; and others again
who had neither inclination nor courage to try
for them. To those who avoid lions from fear of
them, I would say courage can be learnt—it is
a subject for education. When a boy I was
taken to the Crystal Palace and was fascinated
by seeing a man hurl dozens of knives at another
man standing against a door, till the latter's
outline was so lined round with knives sticking
deep into the wood that he was pinned fast
against it, yet so dexterously had this been done
that not a single one of the blades so much
as cut his clothing or scratched his skin. Neither
you nor I probably have the courage to stand that
kind of fire, or to fire those kind of shots. Such
courage as this comes from education and practice.

Presently I shall discuss the question as to
what courage is, and whether lions are courageous. But before I get to lions and chasing them
I want to say something about the Land of the
Lion. I have loved the chase not only for its own
sake, but even more for where it has taken me.
I possess such a store of varied and happy
memories as I would not exchange for all the
wealth and distinction the world can give. Yet
in my youth I believed myself so hemmed in

by circumstances and duties that I thought I should never break through such barriers into the real world beyond. Conventionalities which then looked like a granite wall I have discovered to be a delusion. I have learnt that human beings do not always understand the language in which duty calls, and that by the use of a little force a hole can be made through the thorny zariba of circumstances by which the poor, impounded creature, whether peasant or potentate, may escape to taste of life, of space, of air, and to see the earth, the sun, the moon, and stars as Heaven intended he should know them.

How often have men younger, stronger, wealthier, and with greater leisure than myself asked : " How do you manage to get away; I cannot find time to do these things ? "

I can only reply : " I just book my passage and go." The thing is extremely simple—first determine to go, then take your ticket. I find I always do go when I have done this. As for expense, it need never be more costly to travel or reside in the wilds of Africa than to stay at home, whatever your condition in life may be.

To get there, a working man need not spend more than what he expends over drink and his holidays in a single year. I have met many a white man who has spent years there without as much money as he would spend in a few months at home, and others who lived a pleasant, healthy existence on what they earned by work, by hunting, or by trade. Given a sufficiency of food, a comfortable bed, and an exquisite climate, life is more than tolerable to a liberty-loving man.

If those who have money to spend freely wish to know what it will cost them just to wander once in Africa, with every comfort and provision for camp life, I assert it can be easily done in practically every part of the Continent for £100 a month. The outfitters in many countries will contract to provide for you, in first-class style, for any expedition, for con-siderably less than this sum, including every conceivable necessity in the way of guides, servants, hunters, transport, tents, camp furniture, material, and supplies.

One obstacle that man's imagination sets up is the fancy that the bit of the world in which he lives cannot get on without him. It will some day, and however important he may consider himself, or the community about him may conceive him to be, his importance will dissolve faster than his bones.

Let the man who thinks wealth and social distinction or dissipations the chief prizes in his short life, stay at home—he would not be happy elsewhere. Yet such is even perverted twentieth-century man that he can, as a rule, revert to his primeval home among wild mountains, the wilderness, the jungle, or the bush, and enjoy as much as any one the sweetness of the simple life.

As for myself, I love these months and years in Africa as I do the shade of palms and the sound of waters after the dust and toil of a desert march.

A single visit to the East, to our Colonies, or to any part of Africa is an eye-opener—it is eating of the fruit of the Tree of Life. There is a wonderful world just outside, and so accessible, with countless miles of rich territories where the thrifty and industrious could, with just a little cost to the State, live clean and happy lives, while we are passing law after law, and wasting our wealth in the futile attempt of making over forty millions of fast-breeding folk live comfortably where there is barely room for half the number to exist in decent and healthy surroundings. You go out to Africa to see savages, and you find them only on your return. You will look on the urban populations of Europe with new eyes, and exclaim that the mass of barbarians live healthier and better lives, with fewer wants and less pain, in sweeter surroundings than these.

Your African savage is often picturesque and as often entertaining—he is also generally light-hearted and merry. You pay to see him at Olympia or the Crystal Palace. My European is neither very attractive nor very amusing, but I would also pay to see him in a Somali karia or a Dinka village. You imagine that in these dreadful towns, where you admit your race deteriorates physically, you have a monopoly of the intellectual side of human nature, and talk of the culture of civilization.

After years of travel and sojourn among many native races, Arabs, Berbers, Sudanese, Abyssinians, Somalis, Gallas, Nilotic and Bantu natives of Equatorial and South Africa, I maintain, looking at this array of black, brown, coffee, or paler-coloured peoples, even from the standpoint of intellect, that there is to be found in primitive man of primitive habits, if you know how to look for it, as much intelligence, wit, wisdom, quickness of thought, as among our teeming populations; and though their general capacity for exertion and responsibilities may be vastly inferior, they have an equal endowment at least of those qualities which make for rulers, generals, poets, and lawgivers.

For example, few individuals drawn from the British proletariat could conduct their defence in a court of justice, give their evidence, and cross-examine witnesses with the same skill and acumen as, say, the average unsophisticated kraal Kaffir. Not many of our novelists could jump up and relate a romance fitted to reach the popular fancy of the moment, improvised on the spot, accompanying the recital with an effective display of histrionic and elocutionary talent. This thousands of African and Asiatic natives can do. Could our singers compose their own ballads as they do ? or are the majority of the songs they sing less silly or inane than the

native's chants about his women, and his heroes,
or his camels and his cows ?   With no art
schools and no masters of deportment, natives
have an artistic sense which often prompts
them to the most effective forms in dress and
drapery, the most telling arrangements in colour,
and, in its unconscious simplicity, to the most
perfect grace in action and pose of attitude.

Ah ! but they cannot draw and paint !   It
is true that with "civilization" you find amongst
those less oppressed with toil a yearning for
artistic expression, and that this longing finds
vent in attempts to describe feelings and emotions
with pen in verse or in prose, and to transfer
to canvas with a brush what it has caught in
moments of reversion to nature, or in glimpses
outside the actual environment.   This kind of
art is but a suggestion, a shadow, a memory
of what our race and all races once possessed.

Account for this, please : with no box of
tubes and no camel's-hair pencil, the lowest
type of African aboriginal betrays the latent
faculty of even your art in his quite extraordinary representations of men and animals
in thousands of "rock paintings" on the walls
of the caves and cliffs in which he goes to ground
with the dassies or rock rabbits.   Millions,
moreover, of African natives are under the in-
fluence of the religion of Islam, which discounten-
ances the graven image or any likeness of anything
in heaven or earth.

Why, before he loses the reality in the smoke and fog of "civilization," should the native want to paint, with words or colours, reminders and suggestions of the sunrises and the sunsets, of rivers, of lakes, of forests, and flowers, when all this is what he was born into and will live in, till in the midst of it he dies. Such poetry as the child of nature has in him flows from his heart to his lips; he has no trouble, like laureates, with pens and scratchings out. He refers to knowledge in his head, instead of to bookshelves. As a rule his customs and laws are as suitable to his social and economical condition as ours to our "advanced" state. He can enjoy litigation without maintaining a predatory profession or suffering from the law's delays. He is slow at learning our new doctrine, that the more laws and the more taxes there are, the pleasanter it is for everybody. He is so stupid about this that he will fly at times from British Colonies out of sheer terror of life by rule under a weight of laws and regulations, to take the chance of ill-usage in the Congo Free State.

It may be asserted that the large majority of those who stay at home and work in cities cannot shake themselves free from circumstances which compel them to work there for the livelihood of their families or themselves, nor from responsibilities that are not to be abandoned without a sacrifice of duty. These are inspired by the creditable motives which impel a captain to "stick to his ship." Yet who, on reflection, can deny that myriads of lives are spent in drudgery or in nervous activity, with no real or proportionate advantage to the community, and in surroundings poisonous to the physical and moral welfare of the race. Could but one-half of the wasted energy be turned to work in the open air in other lands of ours, new and healthier ideas of life and happiness would spring up. But how are souls to be converted that grow up in an atmosphere of unwholesome ideals—souls that have come to regard the muddy or dusty pavements of towns, soot-begrimed buildings of cities, and artificial light, food, and pleasure, not only as the necessities but as the joys of existence? How can such be made to see that the primitive man's winding jungle-paths, through a sunlit bush among birds and flowers and butterflies, lead to pleasanter working-places and to sweeter homes than their streets roaring with traffic and reeking with petrol fumes?

In a crowded country it is numbers and confinement which make poverty and dirt. Take the wild boar from his forest and wall him up in a pigsty, and you will in time have, in the place of a brave, sagacious, active, and cleanly animal, a breed of measly-skinned, fat, soft, grunting, squealing beasts, fed on pig-wash, wallowing in filth, and liable to swine fever —Civilization.

Take the Briton and wall him up in towns, and in time . . . well, just look round and see if you have not something similar, and yet no more conscious than the sty-bred pig that there is anything wrong either with himself or his environment—nay, boasting that he is civilized, proud that he is a pig. Whilst millions of public money is forthcoming to maintain a wretched population on the verge of destitution in awful places, not one is ever voted to help our manhood and womanhood to live well-ordered, happy, wholesome lives in our Colonies or to get them there. It would be regarded as preposterous for the State to lend a deserving emigrant a five-pound note that he might achieve a manly independence. Yet the least-deserving " stay-at-home " is to be maintained and pensioned at vast cost out of the public purse.

Average man, if he can know content anywhere, will find it in a climate sweet and pleasant to live in, where Old Mother Earth smiles on his labour and hands up to him his daily bread without much asking, with sufficient shelter wherein to sleep and take refuge from the heat. Does he want much more than to be endowed with an intelligence equal to his duties, the power to be happy when things go well, and to be brave in the days of adversity ? Add that touch of romance, of poetry, and of music which appeals, in its kind, to each race, and the universal gifts bestowed on mankind of natural affection

and hope. Primitive man enjoys this much
—can we better it ? As to whether his own
peculiar terrors and miseries are greater than ours,
who can say ? What have our millions to com-
pensate them for the absence of all this ? It is
a hard task which we have set ourselves, to teach
the natives of Africa to acquire our restless
discontent. We had once two Swahili servants
for more than a year; they both had the run of
the kitchen, but never wanted more than their
one meal of rice a day. When rice was not
obtainable, the difficulty of feeding them was
considerable ; bread and sardines were the only
substitute they would accept, and they longed
to get back to their rice as a Frenchman in the
desert yearns for the flesh-pots of Paris. Yet as
they had been brought up at a mission station
they actually imagined they were civilized.
Poor boys, how could they be with so few wants ?
It was all imagination, for when my wife first
asked, on engaging them, " What food do you
eat ? " they replied, " We are Christians, *we
can eat anything*."

I once introduced a Somali boy for the first
time in his life to a locomotive engine and train.
I knew a native too well to expect any sign of
astonishment,—he does not give himself away
like that,—but I asked him what he thought of it ;
he replied simply, "The white man he can do all
sorts of things, but he has got to die just the same
as a Somali." This boy had come to me from

his karia on the Toyo plains, in his white tobe,
shield on arm and spear in hand ; he became my
personal servant and accompanied me to Algeria,
India, Abyssinia, and England. In the time I
should have taken to acquire one language very
imperfectly, this barbarian, without a soul to
instruct him, unable to read a word, mastered,
with no apparent effort, Arabic, Hindustani,
Amharic, and English, and picked up a smat-
tering of Harrari, Galla, and French. They see
with sharper eyes, they hear with more sensitive
ears, they grasp with more retentive memories—
the result of " savage " education. In the eyes
of Europeans they are all the more barbarians
for this superiority. We think them savages;
what do they think we are—filling up our lives
with hurry and worry, and cudgelling our brains
how we may increase the complexity of our
short existence ?

Perhaps I have over-coloured my general
sentiments in the foregoing remarks. After all,
I am English, and therefore conform, outwardly
at least, to the worship of our national fetish.
I participate, with certain mental reservations,
in the task of teaching the mass of mankind that
it is not to relapse into primitive simplicity—it
must progress, that is—it must raise its eyes
to the great hub of CIVILIZATION, and if its motto
be " Excelsior " the major part of humanity
may eventually reach the ecstatic plane, where
each civilized man may rise each morning by

gaslight, gulp down tea and stale eggs by fog-light, put on his waistcoat with patterns on, seize on his umbrella, rush to a station, read his grey, pink, or green paper in a crowded com-partment, inhaling the breath of others diluted with subterranean fumes, splash through mud, elbow his way over greasy pavements to hail his motor-bus, spend his day at his work under dust-covered lights, in dingy holes, and at the end of his day return much as he came, to supper, quack medicines, and bed. Of course soap, whisky, braces, nail brushes, and many other WANTS are thus created.

I remember a speech of Mr. Chamberlain's, when he urged the importance to the Empire of evoking WANTS among African natives; he wanted Kaffirs to want WANTS—it is good for Trade, and so good for the Empire. In fact, the African native must be *made* to want WANTS; most of all, he must be made to want work. Never fear, he will want his wants all in good time. If we are zealous enough we can hoist him up to our heavenly plane in our patent *ascenseur* a little quicker than he would reach it if he is left to plod his weary way up the long staircase by which we ourselves have climbed.

Sometimes as I have sat under the clean and gentle moon, gazed into the camp fire or blue seas, or looked over sunny plains and purple hills, the dreadful vision has arisen of the civilized crowd at its work, at its luncheons, on

its 'buses, in its trams, trains, and tubes, and
then the image has passed before me of the
Bedawi in their desert, the Somal in their bush,
the Kaffirs in their mountain kloofs, and I have
thought, " Better be any one of these than one
of that crowd." But sympathy and pity are
wasted, success and happiness are measured by
the standard of the corner you are born into
and of the community you live amongst. Verily
if man were born in hell he would mistake it for
heaven. Man's imagination can work miracles.
The crowd's smoke-filled chest swells, its sooty
nostril dilates, its dusty-cornered eye gleams
with the pride of its race. It fights its country's
battles in the newspapers, it is an athlete watching football, it is a " sportsman " when bookies
are bawling the odds or when at night it gets
" all the winners." It lives by proxy, its
romance is in shilling dreadfuls, its travels and
adventures in electric theatres. Yet who dare
say that its life is not sweet. Happiness is
provided for man in the most awful surroundings
where there is love and duty done. But the
great undertaking of the day is the building up
of our Empire. We must have more crowds,
more smoke, more trams, trains, and tubes,
more iron bridges and overhead wires, more
hoarding advertisements in our fields, so that
we may know where to get lung tonic and the
sort of soap to make the dirt drop out, more
sewers and refuse heaps. We must get more

paper and broken bottles in the country, more
rivers running ink, and our lanes well fenced
with barbed wire and railway sleepers to keep
us from straying off the cinder footpaths on to
the fields strewn with pieces of linoleum, tins, and
night-soil. We must have more factories and
mills, or Germany will have as many as we have.
And all the time we must educate our Colonies
to progress, and want the waistcoats with patterns,
and the soap which makes the dirt drop out,
and more of everything we have. In Egypt we
must get the Arabs and natives to give up their
senseless wandering about with tents and camels
without any idea of growing cotton; they must
settle down along the Nile, where our clever
engineers will make more mud for them, even if
they have to bring the water from Central Africa
and harness waterfalls; then they will live in
mud houses along mud roads, by muddy canals,
and hoe mud patches in muddy clothes, and
learn to want whisky and liver pills, bowler hats
and bicycles, and things in time, and breed
more mud-hoers. So governments will raise more
revenue, and cotton-spinners, soap-boilers, and
hoe-makers will get more wealth, and every one
will be better off, and want more and more
things, and so forth and so on, till we reach the
Brummagem millennium. The nation which does
this the fastest will be the greatest, and we mean
to be the first in this race. Instead of the
benighted barbarian watching his wealth wander-

ing on four legs over desert, prairie, and veldt,
we shall see the transfigured being seated at a
roller desk and examining his pass-book under
a gas jet ; instead of gazing in stupid meditation
at purple shadows creeping up red mountains,
and floods of emerald, rose, and violet stealing
over golden plains, he will with educated eyes
look on the unchanging beauty of landscapes in
oil, in rich gilt frames, without having to go out
of doors. Yet perhaps the new and rather
feeble cry of " Back to the land " even in the
form of pigsty in a potato patch (when millions
of acres in the Empire can be had at a half-
penny each), is an indication that the toiling
millions in their smoky dens are unconsciously
looking back in the direction of a former and
more primitive state. I suppose some of them,
if not ready to change places with the Arab in
his tent or the Kaffir in his kraal, might not
turn with contempt from the suggestion of a
settler's life on the veldt.

When I resided in Algeria I knew of a French
general, born an Arab of the tents in the northern
Sahara, who entered the army through the
native ranks, obtained promotion, and then
naturalization which qualified him for the
superior grades, which he attained to, one after
the other, till he was a general of a division. He
became intensely civilized according to Western
ideas ; he had the *entré* to the best European
society, frequented the salons and *cercles* of

Paris, where he had his hotel, and possessed as well a château in the country. The day came when the rule of age retired him from military service. What did he do ? He had lived two existences ; the last as good as the West could give. Off with his hideous European coat, collar, cuffs, top hat, and trousers, one kick and his patent leather boots, with the dust of the West, were off his feet, and into the *burnous* once more ! When last I heard of him he was among his camels and his flocks in the douar of his tribe in that desert which had called him back. I often think of him as sitting at the door of his tent, reflecting on Western ideas of happiness and of what we call success, the horizon of which retreats as it is approached, just as surely as the one of the great desert on which he gazes.

This may seem a strange digression from the track of my lions, but the idea in my head was that in lion lands there are other things to see and think over besides the game. Tough and curious old ideas which will bite the dust there, new thoughts to be born in lion haunts, both quite worth a chase or at least to be examined through a telescope at a safe distance. Let those who denounce my heresies be generous, for mine is the losing cause.

Have I not seen already the dawn of your civilization on the DARK Continent ? The green veldt is being ploughed to give you what you want, the useless beasts and birds are fast being wiped away, the primeval forests echo to the axe, men begin to hoe mud on shadeless flats, the once limpid streams are already running ink, or milky liquid from mines and slimes, Kaffirs wear bowler hats, trousers, and yellow boots. The great " WANT " has arrived, the paraphernalia of Europe is marching in, and there soon will be plenty of billets for doctors and clergy, and dentists and lawyers. By the time that our lion has passed away to remain but the emblem of valour, you will have in some of the more favoured regions even black M.P.'s, as well as the lunatic asylums, sewage-pumping stations, crematoriums, dogs' homes (in every sense), processions of the unemployed, copper-coloured suffragettes, and the native will have his gorgonzola teeth and all the rest of it.

CHAPTER II

ABOUT COURAGE

EMBLEM of valour! These words bring me back to my dissertation on courage. I tried to show that courage is sometimes obtained by education and training. To recognize this is to give any of us who are cowards, hope. I cannot, however, call to mind a single instance of ever witnessing a big-game hunter showing the white feather when faced with danger.

I never envied the man, not that I ever met him, who "did not know what fear is." I know dozens who would face anything in the way of a decent terror, very calmly, and "take it on" either for fun or as duty, or for practice, or with some other excuse, or without any at all. But the poor fellow who knows no fear is poor indeed. Fear is the very essence of pleasure in sport; the real sport begins when there is the excuse to feel afraid. In an old volume of *Punch* you will find a picture by du Maurier (I think), where a German has realized the bearing of this paradox. He has just been instructed by a British sportsman in the mysteries of sport, and exclaims, "Ach! I zee den dat it is ze tanger dat you do like ! You should shoot mit me; ze oder day I shoot mine brudder in ze schtomak." The spice in the tamer amusements of stalking antelopes, deer, goats, and sheep is the dread of being detected and the fear of missing. This is but an imitative fear, yet I can remember when it seemed a very real one, and yielded all those pleasing sensations of trembling and breathless-ness (known as " buck fever ") which result from the real article, and also will now, on occasion, make my heart thump against my ribs. The additional joy in approaching lions, buffalo, or any other dangerous animals is in proportion to your fear of them, or there would be little more pleasure in stopping a lion than in rolling a jackal over. The fun in riding down a jackal is that you have to gallop at top speed on a line unknown. over ground which may or may not be sprinkled with ant-heaps, holes, and cracks, crossed by nullahs and dongas, and that you have at the crisis, when shooting, to leave your reins and trust to your flying horse; it is this element of danger and your fear of it which adds to the enjoyment and excitement of the pursuit. And so in fox-hunting, though a man may love the science of hunting and hound work, if he does not realize the chances he is taking when he rides straight in a screaming run, he knows not the full joys of defeated fears, of pride of horse, and of surviving performances he would not attempt save when the blood of horse and man is " up." The " man who knows not fear " could not enjoy a run with hounds nor a fight with a lion like the man who, though he knows fear, does not show it. He who has never been frightened by a lion must have missed half the sport of lion-hunting. Where there is no fear there can be no courage.

The old meaning of " magnanimous " was brave as well as generous. In confirmation of this statement I refer to Johnson's Dictionary, and to a quotation from Milton therein under the head of " Lion " : " The Fiercest and most Magnanimous of four-footed beasts." I presume " four-footed " enters into this definition so as not to exclude a possible specimen of the human biped, otherwise I cannot account for this qualification and limitation. Milton was expressing a mere platitude when he wrote this, and accepting the general opinion of mankind, based on its experience of this particular kind of beast through the ages. The lion has always stood as the emblem of concentrated courage and terrific power.

If you would flatter a king, you say he is " lion-hearted "; if a man, that he is as " brave as a lion." If a nation desires to impress the world at large without any false modesty it assumes this great cat as its badge, and when so many nations have taken the lion as their pet symbol that the thing begins to get monotonous, the rest fall back on the eagle or bear.

In Africa the proudest title of the Emperor of Ethiopia is " The Conquering Lion of Judah," and the lion is the badge of Abyssinia. Magnanimity in our modern sense has so long been ascribed to the lion that he will remain for ever emblematic of this virtue also, just as great men who, to those who know them least intimately, or when they have passed out of sight, become endowed with sublime attributes. Death oft is the portal to immortal fame, or the *manner* of dying is. Crimes or eccentricities are all forgotten or forgiven if a man dies nobly, whether it be a king on a scaffold or a soldier in the Sudan. The lion dies well, and when the earth no longer sees or hears him, he will be figured with an aureole around his head.

In the learned Job Ludolphus's *History of Ethiopia*, printed in 1684, there are some most charming and most inaccurate descriptions of Abyssinian beasts and birds. In his chapter " Of Four-footed Beasts," he remarks that " As for Wild Beasts, Abyssinia breeds more and more bulkie than any other region of which we shall give a short account, beginning from those which appear most monstrous in their creation." He then goes on to tell us about " such massie creatures " as elephants, " which banquet as upon grass on trees about the bigness of cherry-trees "; about their " horns of which the ivory is made, which grow out of the head and not out of the jaws, and besides that they only adorn the brows of the males, the females, like our does, have none at all "; he describes a female elephant with her " cubb," and how the elephant, " if he be threatened with cudgels, hides his prosces under his belly, and goes away braying, for he is sensible it may be easily chopped off : the extream parts of it being very nervous and tender, which causes him to be afraid of hard blows," and much more of the like. After giving a most excellent description of the zecora (Grevy's zebra), he turns to the lion and says of him : " The lyon, tho' he excel in fierceness and cruelty all the rest of the wild beasts, yet he shews a certain kind of magnanimous respect of man. For he never injures, unless he be ready to famish so that he do not betray his own fear "; and then our friend Job refers the reader to Solinus, who " allows them many marks of clemency : they sooner assail men than women ; they never kill infants, unless pinched with hunger." Solinus indeed seems very generous, but would, in our day, have given grave offence to the suffragettes, and being no doubt a good sportsman who avoided shooting cheepers with his bow and arrow, " allowed " the lion the same sporting instincts. In my search after examples of leonine magnanimity, I remembered the foregoing authority. Personally, I have no particular experience confirming their title to this virtue, beyond a common one of their thoughtfulness in getting out of my way when their

THE QUAGGA (now extinct).

To face p. 24.

presence might be inconvenient. I am less generous than Solinus, and can only allow that, like human beasts, they are more magnanimous after than immediately before dinner.

In Holy Writ the lion appears with " marks of clemency." Daniel in their den must have perceived them. There is also some evidence of their forbearance in the very picturesque story of the Disobedient Prophet. You will remember how the old prophet of Bethel lied unto the prophet who came with his message riding on his ass from Judah, and how he was slain by a lion in the path because he had been so simple as to believe the word of the man of God from Bethel. The story tells how that, after he had been pulled off his ass and killed, some men coming along the Bethel road saw the body and the lion standing by it, and that they ran back and told the liar prophet at Bethel what they had seen, whereupon he bid his sons saddle his ass and then rode off down the track and came upon the body of the other prophet with the lion still standing by it, and also the donkey untouched. Now this lion allowed the old prophet to pick up the body, to fasten it on to the ass, and to take it back to Bethel, where he buried it in his own grave, exclaiming repeatedly at the funeral, " Alas! my brother! " and requesting his sons to put his bones beside his bones when he died. The whole tale as told in the Bible is very graphic, though the moral is a little obscure. However, you cannot expect a higher tone of morality than the highest conception of it that may exist at any particular period of the world's history.

I have known several cases, some of which will be cited later, where by day and night lions have pulled men off horses and carried them off, but they were young laymen on horses, and not old prophets on donkeys. On the whole, judging from Scriptural examples, the lion shows more traces of magnanimity than man.

Look at the story of the valiant Benaiah, the son of Jehoiada, whose valour is instanced in killing a lion in a pit in time of snow. I have tried to picture the deed, yet cannot escape from the impression that the circumstances were on the whole very favourable to the safety of Benaiah. It may be that the valour was displayed in going out in time of snow. What a chance ! Just imagine Benaiah coming out of his hut in the early morning with snow on the ground, and coming on the spoor ; his halt to examine it, his eyes lighting up as with his finger on his lip he exclaims to himself, " Lion ! not hyæna ! " then running back for his spear and tracking the beast without any trouble up the mountain, and at last, looking gingerly over the edge of the rock hole and seeing the half-frozen lion up to his neck in snow right in the bottom at his mercy. The chance of a lifetime ! Few men have had such an opportunity, and few

lions can have had a worse time of it than
Benaiah's.

There are men to-day ready to depose the
King of Beasts from his throne. I understand
that Livingstone was one of the first to foment
this insurrection, and that he declared the lion
to be mean and cowardly, after one had bitten
his arm. I cannot understand why he endeavoured to pull down the lion from off his
pedestal, for from his own account of being
carried off by a lion we are even led to suppose
that he derived some enjoyment from it.

Among the most recent authors, the Right
Hon. Winston Churchill, M.P., writes brilliantly
yet somewhat slightingly of them, but he might
change his opinion on nearer acquaintance.

Has the lion courage ? What is courage ?
I had a Somali camel man well scarred with
tooth and claw of lion. One day when alone
in the bush tending horses at pasture he saw
one of them attacked by a big lion. With no
gallery to applaud and only a horse-hide to
salvage, with just a spear in his hand, he went
straight in and fought a duel to the death with
the lion. Maimed and bleeding he issued victorious from the combat, leaving the great yellow
carcass of his foe beside that of the pony. Did
this boy display courage ?

Listen to what he replies to my wife when
she asks him why he fought the lion, and whether
he was not afraid of being killed :—

" Yes, I was *very* frightened, but I was still more frightened of what they would say in my karia if I went back, if I had let a lion kill the horse and done nothing."

Once in the Gadabursi country a Somali boy, who acted as syce to my second pony, was leading his charge at the tail of our caravan. We camped that afternoon about five o'clock, and when the ponies should have been coming in from feeding at sundown I looked outside the zariba for my white pony and could not see him. I called the headman. " Adan, where is my Fraskiad ? "

" Wery bad nooze," replied Adan, who spoke English, but was shaky about his pronouns. " Lions kill you."

" Nonsense," said I ; " where is the syce ? "

" It is here but too much frightened," was the answer.

My syce appeared, looking very shamefaced. His story ran that as he was leading the pony some little way behind the last string of camels, two lions followed him, and after a short time both sprang on to the pony and pulled him down; that he had then run away, but after a while recollected that there might be a row if he turned up without the pony's halter (the halter was a grass one, worth about twopence), so he had gone back. The lions were still there by the dead pony, but he took the halter off and left the lions near the body.

I was chaffed by my companions for believing the boy, but told him to bring me the halter. He brought it, blood-stained, as it would be likely to be if the pony was killed in the usual way.

An inspection of the scene the next day gave us conclusive evidence of the truth of the boy's account of the end of my little Fraskiad. In this case too the native was more afraid of something else than of lions, which sounds as if I was a perfect terror to my men, when all the time he was only thinking to himself that his honour and his life were rolled in one, and take honour from him and his life was done. Perhaps some Somali bard had taught him this lesson, but more likely not. There have been many instances of natives laying down their lives for their white masters.

I knew a Somali who without so much as a stick in his hand saved Lord Delamere's life with his bare hands. Lord Delamere was down under a wounded lion which had already broken one of Lord Delamere's legs and was crunching it in his jaws. The boy seized the lion's head on both sides, and tugged at him till he dropped his victim and turned and terribly mauled the deliverer. This lion was dispatched by the Somalis the next day, and Lord Delamere set his own broken leg and nursed himself and his boy back to health, if not to soundness of limb. Lord Delamere goes slightly lame, and the boy

is maimed for life, but received a well-deserved
pension from the man he saved.

Now a Somali knows well enough what he is
doing, and must have some strong motive in
courting death to save his sahib's life. I credit
him with the same quick resolution to play the
man which so often distinguishes a European.

A year or so after this event I met in Somaliland an Englishman named Marshall, who had
just had his shikari killed by a lion at Silo. If
my memory serves me right, Marshall was carrying
a loaded single-barrelled rifle, and his shikari
his second rifle. Marshall was in his shirt
without a jacket and had no cartridges, his shikari
was carrying the ammunition for both weapons ;
they saw a lioness slink into a bush, and then
Marshall did a thing that only rash youth would
do. Without getting his shikari close up to him
or taking a supply of ammunition he fired straight
into the bush where he had seen the lioness
disappear, just as if she had been a rabbit at
home. Out she came like a flash of lightning,
straight for the shikari, which was the first thing
she saw, rolled him over, and seized him. Marshall
ran up with his empty rifle and belaboured her
head with the barrel of his gun until she dropped
the man ; then, instead of turning on Marshall
according to the rules of the game, she made off.
In this case the sahib risked his life to save
his black boy, unfortunately in vain. Yet
fortune very often favours the brave.

Here is another example of the cool behaviour of a native and of wonderful presence of mind. This incident, which occurred in June 1909, I will give in the words of Mr. H. Williams, the party chiefly concerned :—

"NAIROBI, *July* 1.

"Mr. Selous and I had joined Mr. M'Millan, but on June 8 I was out alone, having only my two gun-bearers with me, when I saw a lion on the right, about 300 yards away. He was prowling along, and apparently did not notice me, but I could see by the swish of his tail that he was an angry beast. I put up my hand as a signal to my head gun-bearer to come up with a spare rifle, and together we worked closer and closer to the lion. The beast seemed to have no intention of stopping, so I struck one hand on the back of the other. The lion stopped and faced me, probably revolving the question of attack, whilst I, for my part, cogitated as to whether I should shoot or endeavour to get a bit closer. The lion seemed to decide upon retreat, for he turned suddenly and trotted away. I fired both barrels of my ·450 at him, one shot reaching him in the flank. It was only a slight flesh wound, but it paralysed him for the moment, and he sat down on his haunches like a dog. After a few minutes he got up and went into a bit of open bush.

"Not knowing what state the brute might be

in, I made for the big open patch on my left front,
hoping to get a better sight of him. The lion,
however, had been watching me from his retreat,
and at 200 yards distance he sprang out of
the bush and came straight for me at a terrifying
pace. I waited until he was within 60 yards,
and then let him have both barrels. One shot
missed him, but the other lodged in the fleshy
part of his shoulder. The only effect was to
infuriate him more than ever, and I now thought
myself a dead man, for there was no time to
reload, and the gun-bearer was not actually
in reach with the other rifle. I turned and
made for a bush at my right rear, hoping the
beast would rush past me and give me time to
reload ; but it was hopeless, and, turning sharply
round, I stood my ground.

"It was a terrifying sight—the brute's jaws
already open to seize me by my left shoulder and
breast—but with the courage born of despair
I raised my rifle in both hands and struck him
across the side of the head. Almost simultaneously he ducked and seized me by the right
leg, shaking me from side to side as though I
had been a rat. There is no need to describe
what I felt at this moment. Suffice it to say
that my gun-bearer—the pluckiest creature, black
or white, that I have ever read of—came up
whilst the lion was actually mauling me, shoved
the rifle he carried down to me and asked me
how to turn the safety catch. I had sufficient

presence of mind to be able to explain in a second, and the gun-bearer fired. The lion left me and rushed into a bush 5 yards away, giving me time to put two cartridges in my rifle whilst still on the ground.

" Raising myself to fire, I saw that the lion was in the act to spring. I fired off both barrels from my hip at his head, the " boy " firing at the same time, and the brute rolled over dead. I fell back again, and for a few moments half-swooned, for I had lost a lot of blood ; but as soon as the second gun-bearer had come up (no gun with him), I sent him off to find camp and bring back some men to carry me in. With some dressing which I had in my cartridge bag I tried to staunch the bleeding, but could do very little in this way. The muscles were torn open, an artery had burst, and the wounds were everywhere so deep. For an hour I lay there, and then half the camp turned up, and I was carried in on a bed. I shall never forget the agony of that journey. On reaching camp, Mr. Selous and Mr. M'Millan dressed the wounds as well as they could, but that night my temperature was over 105°.

" On the afternoon of the next day—the 9th— I left camp with a man—Judd—in charge of me, and, after three days' travel by hand porterage, I got to Londiani, on the railway, and arrived at Nairobi on the 14th. My leg seemed to be bursting all the time, and the blood was draining

away. I would have given anything for some
morphia. On being brought into hospital, however, I experienced all the ease and comfort
which a first-class doctor and skilful nursing were
able to afford."

The greater the fear, the greater is the
courage of deeds like these. Courage is the
fear of being afraid. A brave deed may be
deliberate or impulsive, it may be thoughtless
or reckless or carefully premeditated, it is as
often dared from the dread of what a man will
think of himself as from alarm at what others
may think of him. Any other kind of courage
is not to be over admired. It is no particular
credit to an individual to possess a quality he
has been endowed with in common not only
with most of his own species, but with dogs and
poultry. Mere bravery of the bravest man is
matched by the bravery of brutes. The soldier
oft repulsed, who, with bleeding wounds, returns
to the charge and fights till his eye dims with
death, is as brave but not braver than the gored
bulldog tossed high in the air, returning to the
conflict time after time, till he has seized his
enemy by the nose, and then never losing his
hold until he is dashed to death or stunned with
blows. By the display of this quality alone
man may attain to the rank of a dog.[1]

[1] This illustration is borrowed from Dymond's essays.

CHAPTER III

OF THE COURAGE OF LIONS

GENERAL SIR FREDERICK LUGARD, having experience of both tigers and lions, maintains the right of the lion to his title of King of Beasts. In support of his view of the superior majesty of the lion he asserts that, unlike the tiger, he "courts no concealment, shirks no encounter, and scorns to run."

I do not dispute his right to his title or his superior majesty, but in the sentence quoted I perceive an over-statement, for though a lion will often stand and regard you steadily when you meet him by day, he will oftener make off at the first sight of you. I should also say he prefers to conceal himself, and when suddenly disturbed generally goes off, and frequently at a gallop. On the other hand, I have seen lions under fire walk off slowly in the most leisurely and dignified manner, halting now and again to look with knitted brows at the pigmies pumping lead at him. Not long ago I was riding through a patch of straggling bush, when two lions got up 200 yards ahead of me; they never stopped to look for a second, but went off as fast as they could. Before I had dismounted and run to a place where I could get a view of them they were 400 or 500 yards away, both going in different directions at a steady gallop like two very long-tailed giant mastiffs. As I watched I saw three more lions jump up, and off they went too, without casting a glance in my direction, though my bullets were chasing them. All these certainly shirked an encounter. Yet the first lions I ever saw in Africa were a group of five or six old ones under a tree larger than any near it in the thorn forest. I came in sight of them at 60 yards, and two of them charged me at sight—but then I had been tracking them for several hours, which makes all the difference. One of these sheered off when I hurriedly fired my first barrel at the leading one, this bullet went " over " at 40 yards, and I had just time to get my second barrel off at 13 yards. My shot sent up a blinding shower of earth into his lowered face, which turned him just enough for him to brush past my shikari; he then whipped round and " came " again. Meanwhile my cool Midgan shikari had put my second rifle into my hand, and I bowled him over; though mortally wounded with one ball and trailing a broken leg, I lost him. For some three hours I tracked him fast and easily, when my boy said it was useless, as he would probably never stop till night. I had given up hope of catching him, and what with six hours tracking in the broiling sun, and my experience with the brute, I found my ardour cooled, but I said to my boy we will go on another half-hour. I was sick of carrying my 10-bore and handed it to him full-cock, and took my Mannlicher, telling him to follow the track, and I trudged wearily on some 10 yards behind. A few minutes after this we went through a patch of high grass under a big tree, and my shikari stepped right on to the lion. This is what I saw : a great, big, bloody lion on his hind-legs, my boy throwing up my big gun to defend himself—the gun held at arm's length going off and the recoil driving the butt into my boy's mouth—my boy falling flat on his back—a dense cloud of smoke (for it was black powder in those days), and then nothing else for a second—then the tail of a flying lion disappearing in thick bush 100 yards away, and " so back to camp,"—a day I remember, with some of the lessons it taught me. There is no " always do " and " never do " about lions, but in my own experience lions will, in nine cases out of ten, at the very least, get away from you if they think they can escape observation or trouble. Most of them have an aversion to man's presence in the daytime, an aversion only overcome, as a rule, by great hunger or unusual nastiness of disposition ; and in disposition they vary almost as much as dogs. But I cannot see that this detracts from their character for courage, as some consider it does. Let us suppose

that the reader has won the V.C. and is sitting
on his lawn under a spreading elm in the heat
of a summer's day, and with eyes half closed
is reflecting on what he has had for lunch or is
going to have for dinner, when suddenly he
catches sight of a lion strolling towards him.
Would you not, brave reader, shin up the tree
or dive into the house by the nearest window ?
Livingstone and Co. might shout " Coward ! "
at you. They would, if logical, write you down
" Coward " too, if when familiar with the sickly
stench of lions a decided whiff of the horrid odour
reached your nostrils, you closed your book and,
with a hasty look round, made off, double-quick,
to the side door. If you now went to your
gun cupboard, and loaded your rifle and watched
your opportunity and shot the unwelcome
disturber of your peace when he was looking
another way, they would if consistent dub you
" mean " as well as cowardly, for, to quote
Mr. Winston Churchill, " such are the habits of
this cowardly and wicked animal." In fairness
however, to Mr. Winston Churchill, I must say
he allows that, when pursued, " the naturally
mild disposition of the lion becomes embittered,"
and " finally, when every attempt at peaceful
persuasion has failed, he pulls up abruptly and
offers battle. Once he has done this he will
run no more." The description of what follows
is so well done, I must give a further extract :—
" He means to fight, and fight to the death.

He means to charge home, and when a lion, maddened with the agony of a bullet wound, distressed by long and hard pursuit, or most of all a lioness, in defence of her cubs, is definitely committed to the charge, death is the only possible conclusion. Broken limbs, broken jaws, a body raked from end to end, lungs pierced through and through, entrails torn and protruding—none of these count. It must be death—instant and utter for the lion or down goes the man, mauled by septic claws and fetid teeth, crushed and crunched and poisoned afterwards to make doubly sure."

In June 1909 I had an example of how necessary it is to kill instantly a charging lion. Near the house I owned on the Mua Hills is a long ridge running down towards the plains ; on the south side of this ridge is a thick covert stretching a mile along the slope beneath fine rocks and boulders. On this ridge are usually countless numbers of kongoni (Coke's hartebeest), zebra, antelopes, and gazelles of various kinds. At certain times of the year lions kill round here almost every night; sometimes they kill in full view of the house in broad daylight. By day they lie hidden in the thickest parts of the bush. We used to know they were there, we heard them grunting or roaring at, and just before, dawn, while at breakfast we saw the vultures and white-necked crows circling over the kills of the night. I often went to the rocks and sat there searching

the bush with my glass, on the chance of seeing
the lions moving into a shady lair for the day,
or sent a boy to watch. I sometimes wandered
in the bush peering into the thick places with
rifle cocked, but generally found this a very
unprofitable amusement.

On the 20th June 1909, after several days'
watching by myself, I got my friend, Mr. R.
Allsopp, and my neighbour, Mr. H. D. Hill, to
give me a hand and see if we could not get rid
of some of these lions, for they had become a
nuisance, being very near the house, frequenting
the main path to it, making it jumpy for every
one of us when taking this track home at night-
fall, and endangering the lives of our boys and
horses when sent to water, morning and evening.
The previous day one of them had killed a
kongoni in sight of the house at dawn, and Allsopp and I had come close on to them when
poking about in the bush.   On the day in question
we determined to try and drive the whole of the
bush towards the plain.   With such force of boys
and dogs as we could muster, I went with my wife
and daughter and our ponies along the crest of
the ridge above the bush, and took up a position
from whence we could scan the whole of the
surrounding plains. Hill, Allsopp, men and
dogs started the drive. We heard their shouts
and watched for some time the impala, kongoni,
zebra, and "granties" pouring out of the covert,
also a hyæna lobbing away, now and again

A Lion Charge.

To face p. 40.

twisting his hideous head round to look back.
Then I saw two big lions slouching along across
open spots in the bush and slanting up the hill.
Before I could get to my horse they were crossing
the ridge about a quarter of a mile off, and by the
time I was in the saddle and my horse going,
they were out of sight. A short gallop brought
me into view of them, indeed I had taken a short
cut that put me nearer to them than I wanted
to be, but they paid little attention. The smaller
of them broke into a gallop and took a long
lead, the larger trotted steadily forward on the
same line, a great hulking brute which shook
all over as he went along. The line was across
ridges and wide bush-sprinkled valleys. As we
rose the first hillside out of the first valley at
a canter, with the heavy lion 150 yards on
my left, I fired a shot from my Mannlicher in
the hope of bringing him to a stand. He
turned and stood for a. moment with a diabolical
scowl on his countenance, back went his ears,
up went his tail as he walked about three paces
towards where I had reined up; before he had
begun to trot, I was in full flight up the hill,
knowing he meant business. He coursed like a
greyhound but gave it up in less than a hundred
yards—he was too fat for that game—and he
resumed his line at a steady trot and paid
me no more attention. I now kept 200 yards
to his right, parallel with him down the slope
into the next valley; on reaching the donga

in the bottom he went into a tiny reed bed and lay down out of sight. I now halted my horse at 120 yards or so, and waited for some of the others to come up. After what seemed a long dose of sentry-go, my gun-bearer on foot with my 10-bore, and Hill and Allsopp on the ladies' ponies, arrived on the scene. Hill carried a ·404 Jefferey cordite rifle, Allsopp a double-barrelled ·450 cordite. We agreed that as it was impossible for a lion to get through this array, we would go straight on to him at once on foot. I was quite sure he would charge us straight, but equally confident he could not reach us; but he very nearly did, and that is the whole point of this tale. We walked up to within nine paces of him, being on ground that sloped downwards to the little patch of reeds which concealed him. There we halted, and a stone thrown by Allsopp brought him out with a terrific grunt—flying straight at us. Bang went all the guns together without any apparent result, and I only got my second barrel off at five short paces—over he went. Now what happened was this : Hill, with that wonderful speed in firing a single-barrelled magazine rifle characteristic of South Africans, got in two, if not three shots ; two struck, one of these hit the lion full in the nose, breaking teeth, cutting along the roof of the mouth and lodging in the base of the skull. This had no effect on the fury and vigour of his charge.

Allsopp's shot only slightly wounded him, and my first barrel struck him where neck and shoulder join; the ball passed under the shoulder blade, raking along his ribs till it stuck in the skin at his hip. All these shots appeared to have no effect on the charge, and might as well have been misses as far as our safety was concerned, though, such was Hill's rapidity of fire, I would not like to say that he could not have got in yet another shot (the last in his magazine) if my second bullet had played me the same trick as my first. I have heard that the nose shot is not a safe one with tigers, but it is a revelation to me that with a powerful rifle a few feet off it is practically useless on a lion,[1] and I suppose one might fire fifty 10-bore balls into a lion's neck without one glancing as my first bullet did. But I call that a courageous lion to face so many standing together and go through so much heavy lead from very powerful weapons fired straight into him at two or three yards' range, particularly when he was fat, gorged, and unwounded.

I cannot subscribe to the epithet " coward " applied to lions, for few will shirk an encounter if they think it necessary. I have observed that lions avoid being followed by men (Cowards !); I have also noticed that men dislike being

---

[1] The late Mr. George Grey, who was fatally injured in 1911 whilst hunting lions with me, hit the charging lion in the mouth and broke his jaw, at 5 yards range, with a ·280 Ross copper-pointed bullet without checking or turning the charge in the least.

followed by lions (Cowards too !); besides, a brave man is not necessarily spoiling for a fight, —some of the bravest I have known were the gentlest and most retiring of persons, but these like lions when they once start, and think they must fight, face fire, wire and water, and throw away their lives, before they will throw down their arms on the field of battle, no matter what are the odds they have to confront.

And what can I say with regard to their conduct in the dark ?   It is true that lions sneak up to their prey and seize their unarmed and unsuspecting victims by the throat or neck, or drag weaker creatures to the ground in assaults from the rear ; but let us be reasonable and consider what would be our behaviour, as courageous men, were all our meals quick of eye and ear and fleeter of foot than we. Is it more cowardly or mean than the way in which we pro-ceed to secure our dinners when we know we cannot catch the said dinner on a fair field with no favour ? And a lion when he is hungry is so very dreadfully hungry—the awful ravening pangs of his inside pass man's understanding ; he does not study how his behaviour may appear to his victims any more than we do when we hide in a grouse butt. What do you say of lions which board railway trains at night and take men out of the windows of the compartments, or of the hundreds of them which leap into crowded villages in the dark among the blazing watch-

fires, to seize their suppers under a hail of flaming
brands, spears, and clubs, amid the yells of men
and the screeching of women; or those innumerable ones which "take on" in mortal combat
such beasts as buffaloes, animals vastly superior
in size and weight, well-armed and, when
embarked on a fight for life, as ferocious
as themselves? No, the lion is a valiant
beast.

CHAPTER IV

OF DANGEROUS GAME

ALL insurrections against the leonine monarchy
are doomed to failure. I have argued the lion's
title on the ground of his superior majesty,
dignity, and courage, but his throne will be
secure by prescriptive right as long as his royal
line continues. Is the lion the most dangerous
of all big game ? This is a question upon which
sportsmen will continue to hold different opinions.
I am convinced, in proportion to the number
of lions killed, there are far more men killed,
fatally injured, maimed for life, and badly mauled
than in the pursuit of any other species of
animal, and that with the sole exception of the
tiger there is no other creature where the immense
improvement in rifles, loads, and bullets gives
man so little advantage over the older patterns of
weapons and conditions of shooting, but I shall
have more to say on this last point later. I
would not like to assert, with my almost total
inexperience of tigers, that if one hundred sportsmen on foot went out, each alone, after one
hundred separate lions, that there would be
more casualties than if the same number of men

of the same quality went out separately after one hundred tigers.

As to facts, tigers are not so much hunted on foot, and as far as I know never on horseback ; they skulk more in jungles and are not constantly encountered in bands or parties. I have no idea what is the largest number of tigers recorded by sportsmen as having been seen together at one time, but I do know that it is rare to see many together in a party, and as many as thirty-three lions have been seen together in one company. Over forty in one troop were seen on the Kapiti Plains in 1911. The Hon. F. J. Jackson (the present Governor of Uganda) saw some years ago twenty-three together near the site on which I built my house. Sir Harry Johnston mentions having seen fifteen in one lot in the Kenia district. I have tracked as many as this together in Somaliland.

Mr. Hume Chaloner, who was with me in British East Africa, saw fifteen in one troop near Embu (May 1909). My tent boy, who was no liar, saw twenty-eight together one day in Somaliland. The Hon. Galbraith Cole told me that two or three years ago, in British East Africa, he was riding alone and not paying much attention to the game around him, when he suddenly became aware that a particular lot of kongoni he was passing through were not kongoni at all, but lions ; he counted twenty-three or twenty-five of them all round him, and remained motionless as the wisest thing to be done under the circumstances. Twenty of them after a short time moved off together, two continued to eye him, and one only made demonstrations of anger, but these also turned and followed the others.

Instances like these could be multiplied almost indefinitely, whilst to see from four to seven in one band is a thing of very common occurrence indeed, and I imagine a very uncommon one in the case of tigers. I think I shall be on the safe side in asserting that nine out of ten tigers killed by Europeans in India are slain from the backs of elephants, from machâns, and other places of safety, or in the company of large bodies of men and parties of sportsmen. Tigers, I should say, deal out far more death to mankind than lions, but then they frequent more populous places and prey on more timid races. As a rule, African natives do not tolerate a man-eating lion, and the community will turn out *en masse* to rid itself of such a nuisance. Some Asiatic peoples, if free from timidity, would refrain from exterminating man-eating tigers from superstition. That a tiger approached on foot is as dangerous an animal as a lion, I well believe, and to follow up a wounded tiger on foot an even more hazardous undertaking. Probably the tiger is endowed with greater muscular activity, quicker moving power, and ability to cover more ground in his bound. His skin is a far more beautiful trophy; but when I come to decide which is the more sporting beast I place the lion an easy first, as best satisfying the standard of sport which I have set up for myself.

In my humble judgment, the risk of serious casualties in hunting elephants, buffaloes, and rhinoceroses on foot is small compared with that of hunting lions and tigers on foot. A man may kill score after score of these animals without coming to grief or even witnessing a fatal accident. Only two men I have known have been killed by elephants in Africa, only one by buffalo, and none by rhino. Personally I am acquainted with no one who has been seriously injured by any of these, whilst it would be difficult for me to count up all the men I have known killed or permanently injured by lions. I am aware that the experience of one individual is poor evidence, yet I think most experienced hunters, if their opinion differed in some particulars, would on the whole agree with me. An elephant under certain conditions and wounds, as also individual wicked ones, can be appallingly dangerous, and where their assailant is disarmed can be most persevering in their vengeance. Occasionally a wounded elephant will hunt a man down most scientifically, circling and sinking the wind till he scents him and then bearing down on him; such a man without ammunition or with a jammed rifle, if he is in a small-bush country or among reeds, high grass, or in dense jungle, is likely to have a very bad time, for wherever he flies or hides he will be discovered by the mighty smeller-out.

I have heard of some marvellous escapes from elephants. Mr. Victor Cavendish told me that on his journey through Somaliland to Lake Rudolph, when he shot a large number of elephants, he on one occasion wounded an old bull, which thereupon took up his stand on fairly open ground behind a bush. Cavendish's shikari told him the elephant was going to charge, and he made haste to reload his empty barrel. He opened the breech, ejected the empty case, and put in another cartridge, but he could not get the cartridge home in the chamber; he tried force, but failed—then tried with all his might to draw it out, but in vain, and now the elephant bore down on him while he struggled with the cartridge which jammed his rifle open. There was nothing for it but to fly; he saw that there was about 100 yards of open to cover on foot before he could reach the only refuge in the bush which could possibly give him time to deal with the refractory cartridge. Long before he had reached this shelter the huge head of the elephant over-shadowed him—he flung himself on one side on the ground and lay motionless as the great monster with all his "way on" thundered by; then round swung the elephant and came for him—down on to its knees it went, prodding at him with its heavy tusks; but before it had touched him Cavendish had wriggled under the elephant's chin, out of reach of the tusks and out of sight of his little eyes. From this time for some twenty minutes or more the elephant endeavoured to pound him with his knees, but never fairly " got him." Meanwhile Cavendish's shikari had run back to his master's pony and syce, and had got another rifle and returned. He naturally believed his sahib had been dead some time, nevertheless he approached the elephant and pumped bullets into him; then the elephant got up and moved off about 70 yards. To the astonishment of the Somali boys, the corpse on the ground got up and came towards them with not so much as a broken bone, and a few days' rest in camp saw him practically recovered from the bruises and contusions he had received. If the fast shuffling trot of an elephant may be called " flying " it may be generally conceded that they almost always fly from every trace of humanity. The merest whiff of a man suffices to stampede a whole herd. When an elephant is cornered, or surprised and wounded, and, with trunk upraised and ears set out like sails, he bears down screaming upon his enemy, a shot in the chest or head generally (I very nearly said always) turns or stops him, at any rate with a modern elephant rifle. The lion has keen sight, possibly the most perfect of any creature, but the elephant, like the rhinoceros, has considerable difficulty in seeing. Once with the wind right but with impassable water between me and some fine tuskers, I tried for a long time to attract their attention, even firing several shots in their direction; they sometimes moved a little after they heard the shot, but evidently could not make me out, though I was standing in full view on the top of a very large ant-hill.

Again, elephants are usually shot at very close quarters, say from 5 to 30 yards distance, and provided the wind is right, and the huge beast carefully stalked, a very deliberate and accurately fatal shot is comparatively easy. When it is all over he is a bit of a ruffian who does not feel remorse at the sight of one of these sagacious, magnificent monsters, which may have taken Nature near a hundred years to furnish with his size and ivory, laid in ruins at his feet.

Nearly every sportsman who comes out to British East Africa for big game kills several rhinoceroses, not a few of these visitors return home without ever having the chance of killing lions; yet many are the men killed or mauled by lions, and very, very few are those injured by rhinoceroses.

The powerful rifles of the day are wonderfully effective on rhinoceros but give little advantage, if any, over old-fashioned weapons or even small-bore rifles in the desperate charge of a lion. Personally I have never known a single instance, where a rhino charged a man armed and ready for him, when the rhinoceros did any damage at all. Though rhinoceros often charge, I am quite

certain that many so-called rhino charges are
not charges at all, and, as often as not, when a
rhino jumps out of his bed in a thicket with a
snort and a rush that is alarming (generally the
result more of terror than anger) his only instinct
is to get clear of the bother as fast as he can.
On such an occasion I have stood stock-still at
the " ready " without firing, and though he has
charged out he has gone careering past without
paying me the slightest attention. A friend of
mine told me that when on safari down the Tana
River, his party disturbed on a march of several
weeks over one hundred rhinoceros; of these
only one charged the safari, and this happened
when they were in horseshoe formation and he
charged straight through the porters. However,
it does not much matter whether his intentions
are innocent or otherwise if you happen to be in
his way, and often men and camels have been
sent flying and much damage has been done by
a rogue or a terrified rhino.

Mr. Relly of Nairobi gave me an amusing
account of seeing a rhino charge a train he was
in, on the Uganda Railway, and how he twice
went headlong at the carriages, striking the foot-
board each time and then retiring at a trot
towards the hills with a very bloody snout, like
any other anarchist running up against civilization. You do not want to get in the road of a
beast which tries to butt over railway trains.
Yet I hold to my opinion that the rhinoceros,

either white or black, if inquisitive is seldom aggressive, and only a small proportion of his kind is really vicious. These latter are more frequent near places where they are liable to be disturbed. The rhinoceros likes to spend his harmless life as far from the white man as he can.

As for buffalo, they are certainly dangerous game, my own impression is that after lions and tigers they and elephants are the most dangerous adversaries a sportsman can engage. The best authorities are not agreed as to how dangerous buffaloes are. I have met many men whose opinions are worth having, who count the buffalo as the most dangerous of all big game. Opinions on this point are largely formed according to the district and kind of country where experience has been acquired. Selous declares : " I do not consider the Cape buffalo—and I have had an immense experience of these animals, and have shot well over two hundred of them, mostly on foot in every kind of surroundings— to be a naturally vicious or ferocious animal." A man who knows so much about the beast as this is not one to dispute with ; at least I am in no way qualified to argue the question. The late George Grey, with a great experience of them, held the same opinion. The Hon. F. J. Jackson, with a long experience in Equatorial Africa, says : " I consider it the pluckiest, and, wounded, the most cunning and savage of all game that is considered dangerous." I will only add that it appears to me that had the man who has killed over two hundred buffaloes on foot killed two hundred lions on foot in the daytime he might be considered fortunate to have survived, and at least would not be able to declare that the lion was naturally not " a vicious or ferocious animal."

As far as Africa is concerned, there remains no other game whose claims to the character of dangerous are worth examining in relation to the lion, unless it be possibly the panther. I do not allude to the leopard, which is only a very big cat, which flies at a man readily and viciously on very slight provocation, and at times without any ; but which after all does not brain him with blow of paw or crunch big bones up between great jaws. The leopard is an animal you can brain with a club or strangle with bare hands, and which bites and scratches in a very nasty way, as I have seen it do, yet apart from the risk of blood-poisoning there is little danger to life and limb in hunting them. Scientific naturalists refuse to recognize a difference between panthers and leopards, yet I venture to declare that there is no comparison between the great dark panthers of North Africa and the common leopard, either in appearance, size, weight, or power to inflict injury. I have seen panthers nearly as large as lions, with immense arms and muscles, and panther skins as large as lion skins.[1] The

[1] I read in a French newspaper that a panther had been killed this year (1913) in Algeria which measured, before being skinned, about 8 feet 10 inches (2 m. 75 cm.).

panther is still to be found in the Atlas Range, a few in the mountains of Somaliland, and no doubt elsewhere in Africa. There was one I sought for in vain which had claimed many victims among the natives near the Jerato Pass in the Golis Mountains; he had haunted the Gan Libah for some years. The Somalis distinguish the panther by the name of " Orghobie " from the leopard, which they call " Shabel." The Arabs of North Africa hold the panther in more dread than the lion. In old days when the panther was still ubiquitous in the Atlas my Arab hunters told me panthers very often became man-eaters, that they would frequently, in a way very rare in the case of lions, fly out from above on to men as they walked on mountain tracks, and that they were often as large as lions; that whilst it did not matter so much approaching a lion from below, it was a most dangerous thing to go up-hill to a panther.

Leopards do, however, stalk and attack natives, and not infrequently carry off women and children. I was once stalked by a leopard whilst dozing in the shade of a candelabra euphorbia tree, in the Gadabursi Mountains, after a fruit-less morning after greater kudu. My three boys were sleeping under another tree 100 yards away. I had my ·256 rifle laid across my knee, my feet on a little ledge of rock, below my boots stretched high grass down the steep side of a mountain gully, and an upland breeze fanned me pleasantly. I was roused by a soft purring grunting, and half opened my eyes and instinctively turned the safety off my rifle; in Africa one learns without effort the habit of sleeping even by night with one eye open, as it were. I gazed sleepily without the least apprehension of danger at the waving yellow grass in front of my feet, and saw what I thought was the top of a cat's tail twisting and turning above the surface of the grass 10 feet below me. Then it suddenly struck me that this cat's tail was exceedingly long and marked uncommonly like a leopard's, and also getting uncommonly near me—in fact I realized I was being stalked up wind; at the very moment that the situation flashed on my brain, the top of the leopard's head and eyes rose slowly to the top of the grass exactly over the toes of my boots. I whisked the rifle round with the muzzle within an inch or so of its eyes, and fired. Up went the leopard in the air, as I thought dead. I jumped up and looked at the bent grass at my feet where the leopard appeared to fall, but no leopard was there. The boys ran up to me, and for an hour we searched the gully, but never so much as found a drop of blood. What happened I do not know; a miss was difficult to believe, for though I had no time to put the rifle to my shoulder the muzzle was practically touching its nose. The only explanation I could suggest to myself was that the bullet glanced off the skull above the eyes, which would be almost in the same plane as my rifle when his eyes met mine above him.

Leopards will stalk people asleep, but the cowardly hyæna will do this; while a leopard seizes by the neck or throat, the dirty hyæna grabs at the face. We had a Somali cook, Ali Saha, now dead, who had half his face taken off in this nasty way by a hyæna whilst he slept. Hyænas are very bold at night; I have several times known them come right into tents. I recollect a hyæna carrying a saddle out of one of our tents while the occupant slept, and eating practically all of it but the stirrup-irons. This is preferable to awakening without a face, or only so much of one as might cause you yourself to be mistaken for a hyæna.

Once in the Danakil country my wife woke me up, calling to me in a whisper, "There is something in the tent; is it a lion?" It was a bright moonlight night and our tent door was wide open, but the tent, being double-roofed and under a big tree, was dark inside. I always slept with a 10-bore gun, loaded with buckshot, close to my hand. I seized this and raised myself slowly in bed, but could see nothing.

"I saw it come in," whispered my wife, "and it stood in the doorway." As she spoke I saw a large beast standing in the doorway; as I moved my gun it bolted out and I ran to get a shot. As it emerged out of the shadow of the tree I just saw that it was a hyæna, but he never gave me the chance of a shot. However, my wife's alertness saved our faces — moral, always travel with your wife.

A friend of mine in East Africa had, not very long since, a nerve-shaking experience at night. He was travelling with a troop of ostriches and was sleeping on the ground close to the tent so as to be able to guard them better. In the middle of the night he awoke with a horrible sensation, and opened his eyes to find a huge brute standing over his body breathing an awful breath and glaring in his face. What it was neither he nor his friend in bed within the tent had any idea. Their screams and shouts frightened it away, but it was long before my friend could sleep comfortably again in the open. I expect it was a hyæna, though my friend rather inclines to the opinion that it was a lion. The only description of the beast's face I could get from him was that it was too awfully terrible and hideous for words !

Some people regard wild dogs (*Lycaon pictus*), often called the Cape hunting-dog, as dangerous, but the instances are rare of their having attacked men. I have never seen them attempt it, but know of two cases, related to me by eye-witnesses, both of whom I regard as absolutely reliable, in relating what they had seen.

Some years ago one of the Sabi game rangers in the Barberton district told me, that as a certain Mr. Colman was making his way over the veldt near the picturesque kopjie of Logogot he heard the screams of a Kaffir, and, riding on to see what was the matter, he beheld five wild dogs attacking, in a most determined manner, a Kaffir who was defending himself with a white cloth which he was waving and shaking at them. The other case was where my informant saw a Kaffir on a path in the bush carrying the head of a freshly beheaded cow in his hand, when a wild dog suddenly rushed out on to the track and snatched the head away from the native.

As for myself, I would rather meet, as I have frequently done, a pack of wild dogs than a troop of angry baboons. These last have given me as good a scaring as ever I have had, and I have seen the boldest man come into camp shaken after an encounter with these dog-faced gentlemen.

Wild dogs [1] do not eat carrion as a rule, they kill for themselves and in a very wholesale way. At the same time, I have seen them eating dead rhino, on returning to the carcass of one shot the previous day. I have seen hundreds of wild dogs, and always in packs—rarely less than five together, and more often from ten to forty. In the Transvaal I have shot wild dogs with the prevailing colour dun, blotched, spotted, and striped with brown, legs and feet spotted with white as well, and white tip to tail; such a skin

---

[1] I am referring only to the *Lycaon*, and not to the quite distinct races such as the Abyssinian wolf (*Canis simensis*), etc.

I have had measuring, unpegged over all, *i.e.* from tip of nose to tip of tail, more than 5 feet. This is the common type, with variations in the markings, of *Lycaon* in South Africa.

Abyssinian wild dogs appear to me to be as large, if not larger, the Somali ones smaller, whilst the British East African sort is so much smaller and the prevailing dark brown so distinct that even a short distance off he looks like a little black dog with a white tip to his tail. All these brutes are most destructive and will at times kill the larger antelopes, but more frequently hunt the smaller buck, duikers, steinbuck, modaqua, gazelles, and the like. They are particularly fond of impala.

In Abyssinia I once followed a pack about fifty strong, and every few hundred yards, during a pursuit of some five miles, I came upon the remains of some small buck, a hoof or bit of skin in the trampled and blood-stained grass, which they had killed as they fled before me, and this in spite of the fact that several of their number had my bullets through them. Wild dogs can *look* very alarming. I have stood with thirty or more of them in lines in front of me at about 40 yards distant, jumping in the grass to get a better view of me and barking. Being without a boy I felt very uncomfortable till they departed, which they did after I had laid out four or five of them. However, they cannot be classed among dangerous game in any further sense than that if you were to come across a starving pack (a very unlikely thing), they might behave in the same way as their more powerful relations the wolves or their cousins the hyænas.

The following classification of Wild Dogs (*Lycaon pictus*) has recently been attempted: I think it may require further additions and some alteration when more specimens are collected and compared :—

1. *Venaticus*.—This name has been given to the South African type. It is distinguished by the prevalence of orange yellow over the back, the partially yellow backs of the ears, the large amount of yellow on the underparts of the body, and the whitish hairs on the thoral ruff.

2. *Mozambiqus*.—The Mozambique type exhibits an almost equal distribution of yellow and black both above and under the body. The backs of the ears and the throat ruff are black. The whole coat has less white in it than that of *Venaticus*.

3. *Lupinus*.—The East African variety is distinguished by being much darker; the yellow is reduced to a minimum.

4. *Somalicus* is described as being smaller than the others, shorter in its coat, with less powerful teeth, and generally dark in colour. From my own observation I cannot confirm the description of the Somali wild dog as smaller than the East African. The British East African wild dog in the upland districts is the

smallest *Lycaon* I have met with. The Transvaal and the Galla or Abyssinian varieties are the largest I have seen.

5. *Zuluensis.*—This type is profusely mottled on the back with white as well as yellow and black. The fur is long and coarse, the backs of the ears are blackish, and the underparts tricoloured. The tail, which in some varieties has a small tip of white, has about half its length white. (Probably there is little difference between the Zulu and Transvaal varieties.—A. E. P.)

6. *Sharicus.*—The Boyd-Alexander expedition came upon a new variety of *Lycaon* in the Shari region, which was given this name. The account of this *Lycaon* by Boyd-Alexander in his *From the Niger to the Nile* is hardly sufficient for identification purposes. It is merely this : " Skin a mixture of yellow, black, white, and grey, with bushy tail."

Hyænas are utter cowards, but when they get together in packs of over a dozen, as they occasionally do, they may sometimes be dangerous. I have seen a few hyænas make a leopard drop a sheep at once; and the most diabolical row I ever heard in my life was one night, south of Hargaisa in Somaliland, when a crowd of hyænas attacked a lion. The Somalis say it is not uncommon when a number of hungry hyænas get together, for them to kill a lion on his victim. Hunger will drive man or any other carnivorous

creature to desperate deeds—yet the hyæna must
be writ down a coward of the cowards.

The only occasions outside a zoological
garden when I have heard hyænas laugh were
on the two I have just referred to, and I imagine
the laugh was entirely on their side both times.

To return to wild dogs for a moment. An
acquaintance of mine, a very fine type of the
South African low-veldt colonist and of Scottish
birth, named William Saunderson, a man as
observant as he was intelligent, told me he had
tried to tame wild dog pups, and succeeded,
but, as they never lost their very offensive smell,
and always reverted to temporary ferocity over
any meat, he gave them up. He also found
them a nuisance when he had them out shooting
with him, for they would always hunt on their
own and apart from the other dogs. The last
ones he kept he allowed to eat a dead cow, and
they ate the meat till they literally burst, and
thus he was rid of the lot, Death coming to them
in his most attractive and sweetest aspect.

The bitches drop their litters of five or seven
cubs in a group of ant-bear holes or some such
earths, and the families will all dwell together.
The mothers, however, do not live with them, but
lie outside and hunt, returning from time to
time. They feed their pups by vomiting outside
the earths. Saunderson was absolutely certain
of this, and in his experience there were generally three or four families together. He asserts

that hyænas do the same, but that, as far as he could tell, the female seldom produces more than one cub, which is fed in the same dainty manner. If this is so, and I do not doubt it, it adds another point to the apparent ones of similarity between *Lycaon* and *Hyæna*. The striped hyæna (*H. striata*) is the only one I have ever seen in North Africa, and I do not know how far north the largest of the hyænas, the spotted one (*H. crocuta*), ranges, but as the cave remains of Europe, including those of Yorkshire, are said to include remains of *crocuta*, I presume this species was distributed all over Africa at one time. It would be well to have an authoritative statement as to whether the striped hyæna (*H. striata*) of the Atlas region is identical with that of Somaliland and of Equatorial Africa. I know all these, but have omitted to compare the skins and skulls of the specimens I have killed. Judging by what I have killed myself, I am inclined to think the North African type altogether larger than the East African one and somewhat bigger than the Somali one.

The authorities affirm that *striata* is not found in South Africa, only the brown hyæna (*H. brunea*) and the spotted (*H. crocuta*). I believe the striped to be very uncommon south of the Equator, though I have shot one near Sultan Hamoud in British East Africa, and know of two that were poisoned near Lion Kopjies in the Transvaal at kilometre 70 on the

Selati Railway in 1887. The brown hyæna ranges as far north as Kilimanjaro, if Sir H. H. Johnston saw one, as he believes he did, on that mountain. The striped hyæna is far more aggressive in North Africa than elsewhere, frequently killing donkeys, mules, and occasionally horses, seizing them in the flank or belly and disembowelling them. All the Hyænidæ are mischievous in this sort of way where carrion and kills are scarce.

Even the little aard-wolf inflicts considerable damage on sheep and goats in Somaliland, and I believe also in South Africa his habits in this respect do not commend him to the farmer. I may add that with regard to the spotted hyæna there are still persons, generally well informed, who maintain the old superstition that the spotted hyæna is hermaphrodite, which of course is absurd. The sex is somewhat difficult to distinguish by external evidence, save when the female has young.

The cheetah or hunting leopard belongs to a separate division of the Cat family, and cannot be considered in the least a dangerous animal. I have seen many killed, and I have ridden down a considerable number myself as well as shot them on foot. I have frequently gone up to them on foot when wounded or at bay, and never seen them make any attempt at defence beyond growling and snarling. The African variety differs hardly at all from the Asiatic, save that its pretty spotted coat is a little more woolly in its texture. The cheetah on sound and open ground gives a good run when pursued on horseback, but is almost invariably ridden down. They destroy a great deal of game and will kill large antelopes.

I once shot a serval attacking a hartebeest (*Bubalis swaynei*) bull, which I also shot with my second barrel, so I can well believe a pair of cheetahs have been seen to kill a greater kudu. Cheetahs often hunt in couples, though I have seen quite as many alone as in pairs. They seize an animal by the throat and hang on like bulldogs till it drops. They have several cubs, usually three or four in a litter, with very long, woolly, darkish coats. A big cheetah stands within an inch or so of 3 feet high, measures over all 7 feet in length, of which length the tail takes up more than a third. They are long on the leg and light and lithe of body. It is not true that they have dog's claws—their claws are as sharp as a cat's, as I have known to my cost when handling young ones, which are very easily tamed, besides their claws are at least partially retractile. Cheetahs have a very singular whistling bird-like note. Sir Harry Johnston says that the cheetah of South Africa is red spotted, but this is not so; they do not differ in colour in any way from all the other cheetahs in different parts of Africa which I have seen, and, like them, are spotted with dark brown spots on a pale buff or cream-coloured ground—what the casual observer would probably call black spots on yellow ground. Slight variations in colour are found among all species of animals and in all localities. Albinism or melanism may occur in any species. Probably there is no member of the Wild Cat family so liable to colour variations as the leopard. I have never seen or heard of an albino leopard, but black leopards are by no means uncommon in either Africa or Asia. I do not know either of a white or truly black lion ever having been seen or killed.

CHAPTER V

ON a previous page the opinion has been expressed that of all big game the lion is the most sporting beast, at least so I judge it by the standard I set up for myself. I am not sure that pig-sticking in India would not take the first prize, and pig-sticking in Africa run lion-hunting close, if it came to the votes of sportsmen (who have had a fair innings at all) as to what was the best sport. If I were asked my own opinion, I should say that a really first-class run with foxhounds beats everything. Still we can hardly call a fox " big game," and I don't quite know where to put the pigs.

The wild boar of Europe is big game, the smaller pig of India is as plucky and bold as any in the world, and a trifle more active by all accounts. The wart hog and bush pigs of Africa can be formidable at times, and any one who had not seen how the former can stand up and go over a country, as well as charge and fight, would hardly credit what a sporting animal even a wart hog can be ; yet I do not think I shall be far from the mark if I say that about nine out of ten sportsmen, if the choice were given them, would choose the day after lion rather than the day after pig. At any rate, the lion comes up to the top of the standard by which I measure a sporting beast. The reader shall have this standard to criticize, condemn, or approve of. My definition of " Sport " is fair competition with man or beast for the mastery as a recreation. Where wild animals are concerned, the competition, to be fair, must have for its field of action their natural haunts.

In reflecting upon the constituents of field sports, I have come to the conclusion that there are four principal ones, and that when all these are present the sport is entitled to be termed true sport :—

1. Absolutely wild game the object of pursuit.

2. Nature's field for the action.

3. Physical exertion.

4. Exercise of skill.

By this standard there is no true sport in attacking or pursuing any animal anywhere, save when it is absolutely free in its natural haunts. The true sportsman delights in matching his own endowments of instinct, endurance, sight, hearing, and observation, also his acquired knowledge and skill, against the endowments and acquisitions of his competitors. Nature bestows on some animals rapidity of motion, endurance, and concealment, agility in climbing, sensibility of sight, smell, and hearing; on others a size, strength, and armament for attack or defence which would make either chase or combat futile for man, did he not call to his assistance weapons, the product of his own invention, and enlist in his cause the services of horses and dogs or of birds of prey, bred and trained by his own efforts and skill, to suit his purpose. Almost all sport has become so artificial in the British Isles, and is pursued under such bastard conditions and regulations, that it is only a few of the field sports which reach this standard; even in the British Possessions in Africa a man cannot now go where he will, shoot what he likes, and regard himself as having secured by his own enterprise a monopoly over the big game of whatever vast territory his own sweet will has led him to explore. These delights belong to a past and cannot now be experienced. However, at home the four constituents named may still be found present in wild-fowling, in grouse, partridge, woodcock, and snipe shooting, and in hunting and deer-stalking. In inferior or bastard sports, such as tame pheasant and tame duck shooting, or the shooting or coursing of rabbits and hares in earth-stopped warrens or enclosed grounds, at most the second and fourth may be present.

In the case of coursing and shooting in enclosures only the fourth, and no great amount of that as a rule can be detected. These latter forms of diversion, with pigeon-shooting and the like, fall into a low class near badger- and bull-baiting—less brutalizing but more cruel. The only point in which such pursuits can claim any superiority over a cock or dog fight is that they possibly admit of a superior exercise of skill.

The man who devotes himself to a sport in which the exercise of his own skill is the only factor present, seems hardly to have acquired thereby any title of " sportsman." At best it is a recreation. Such amusements as tame pheasant and duck shooting are indulged in by thousands who on other accounts are rightly dubbed sportsmen.

To fish fairly in river, loch, and sea; to hunt fairly with hounds or rifle or gun on foot or on horseback; to stalk and climb after wild sheep, goats, chamois, mouflon, and deer; to pursue big game,—all these satisfy the conditions laid down.

True sport increases in quality as the game and its haunts are more truly wild, and yet more and more as the element of danger and the mimicry of war enter into it. I do not enter into the bearing of the question as regards competitive contests between men—such as prize-fighting, wrestling, athletics, football, polo, flat and hurdle-racing, and steeple-chasing—further than to say that the men who take part, the men who give and take the knocks, the men who play and the men who ride, most certainly deserve their title of sportsmen, for these contests bring into play in a very high degree most of the constituents of sport. On the other hand, those who bawl and take the odds and all such have not an iota of a claim to any fragment of such distinction. You cannot be a sportsman by proxy.

The players of games from cricket downwards are in a category apart. The " image of war," which authorities from the time of Xenophon to that of John Jorrocks consider sport must be in some degree, is not so easy to discern in them. Such games are manly pastimes and recreations rather than sport. The man who plays games for pay is in the lowest class of all. This kind of thing has become the prostitution of recreation.

The fascination of sport is dependent to an enormous extent on the field of action. The moor and the loch, the rivers and streams, the valleys and plains, the mountains and crags, the wilderness and the desert, the jungle and bush truly belong to the true sportsman and to him alone. Sport is the only medium which will convey real intimacy with them. Others may enjoy acquaintance with them, but in the sportsman's ear alone does Nature whisper her confidences, and to his eye alone does she discover all her charms and all her moods and tempers.

Others may learn much, see much, enjoy much, but the most and best is known to the man who quits his bed before sunrise, who

spends his nights as well as days by the month
and the year on mountain-ranges, in forests, and
in the wilderness, who bears heat and cold and
hunger, thirst and toil, for love of her; and is
pushed by his passion down into the abysmal
depths of Himalayan gorges, African kloofs, or
American cañons, or led up to snowy peaks, to
realms of eternal ice, or over the sun-withered
wastes of the earth, to visit the utmost refuges of
beast and bird.

The artist is his only rival in his courtship,
the only competitor for the bliss of a sportsman's
paradise. The best artists have something of
the sportsman's instinctive longing to see, to
touch, to handle, and the best sportsmen have
something of the artistic temperament. Yet
when I think of it, where is the artist in literature or painting who, like innumerable sportsmen,
despising wealth and fame, have wandered off
alone to spend all their years in Nature's wilds,
finding there alone what can satisfy their love
of her delights ?

Lion-hunting meets all the requirements of
sport. The lion is a wild beast in Nature's
wildest haunts—he calls for exertion in his
pursuit and skill for his defeat. Many wild
creatures lead us into grander scenery.

To my mind nothing compares with the hunting of wild goats and wild sheep (in which I
include many species of these families—chamois,
mouflon, ibex, and the rest), a sport which calls

forth the highest efforts of skill as well as of endurance, the whole craft of hunting in the most magnificent and terrible places on God's earth. I would rather have hanging on my wall the head of an old markhor than that of the best lion I have ever seen, all the more because I know the time has now gone by when I could stand the work necessary to win this prize.

A high pheasant may require as much skill to kill neatly as a charging lion, but it does not matter so much if you miss him or only take his tail off. When you are, as a friend of mine calls it, " closing with " a lion you feel you are engaged with the arch-enemy of man and beast, and that only one of you may come alive out of the fight. This is the spice which makes the pursuit of lions so attractive. The lion's mien, his eye, his voice proclaim him a royal antagonist; his teeth, his claws, his mighty arms, his strength, his size all vouch for his being a very formidable one.

OF TERROR

I have known fear often, but true terror only once, and though it has not very much to do with lions, a description of how I was literally terrified out of my senses may serve as a warning to others of what not to do when out lion or any other kind of hunting. The experience has been a lasting lesson to me. To any but those who have been in the same position the story may appear both ridiculous and trivial. To my companions at the time it never appeared as more than as an everyday incident to travel; not so to me. Any one who has been truly lost alone knows what true terror is; there is no other kind of fear like it—the horrible anxiety I have felt once or twice in the Sahara when the guide has confessed himself off the line, the close adherence to which means life or death, is nothing to being lost alone. In the course of an hour or two I confess to having been reduced to a condition when I could neither trust my eyes nor use my reason.

Lions were the indirect cause of what happened to me on this occasion. I have been lost in the bush by day and by night for longer or shorter periods, but save on this one always in the company of one or more natives; this time I was by myself, in an uninhabited country and a day's march from any water, and even its direction quite unknown to me. We were marching through a waterless, hilly country, making a course about due north, but our caravan of camels had to wind in and out of the ravines and valleys which spread like a great network over a vast region. We generally meandered along dry-stream beds.

One evening as we were pitching camp, I looked up to the bush-crowned crags above us, as the sun was setting, and saw a hyæna gazing down from the edge of a cliff. He looked grim and black against the red west, which shone through the leafless thorn trees on the edge. I picked up my rifle and clambered up the side of the ravine, but had hardly started on my ascent when the hyæna made off. I hurried up, and when I reached the top saw the hyæna again, lobbing away through the trees. I followed him a few hundred yards in the hope of getting a shot, but he disappeared down another ravine to the west. I went to some rock terraces overlooking this gully, but saw the hyæna no more. Just as I was about to turn back I noticed three objects, which looked very large among the stunted trees, about half a mile away on the other side of the little valley. They were moving along in single file between me and the sinking sun. At first I thought they were wild donkeys, of which there were a goodly number in some parts of the country, but yet hardly likely to be quite so far from water as this. Then I saw that they were three lions walking steadily along. It was too late to think of going after them, and I had not ammunition enough to attempt it with my ·256 rifle, so I returned to camp and told my shikari what I had seen, and suggested trying to find them in the morning.

At dawn we broke up camp, and while my two shikaris were giving a hand in taking down my tent, I placed on the ground my water-bottle and ammunition for the day for them to pick up, and thought I would just go and see if I could track the lions at the place where I had seen them the evening before. If I found they could be spoored, my intention was to return for my boys and then follow them up; it was not more than three-quarters of a mile to where I had seen them. I had five cartridges in my ·256 rifle and ten in my pocket. When I got to the top of the cliff the sun had just risen behind me. Camp and the sun were in a direct line. I soon reached the place and found the spoor. This I followed in and out of the bush, down one little valley and up and down another, across and up another and so on, to some rocky terraces, where after casting forward and round, I gave it up and was going to turn back. Just at this moment I spied a herd of gerenuk (*Lithocranius walleri*), and I thought I would stalk them and see if there was a good male among them; I got up to them and saw they were all females. I then realized that I must hurry back, as the caravan would already have started. I instinctively looked up at the sky to make a guess as to how long I had been away, the sun in Africa being always a handy and correct time-keeper. I looked for the sun above the bush on my right hand—to my horror it was glaring at me on my left. I stood rooted to the spot. I had intended to bear away straight to my right, having a general faith in my bump of locality. In my mind camp was most certainly on my right, and beyond it ought to be the sun in the east, but there was the sun in the west. Though my reason declared what I held was west was really east, and what I felt was south was really north, I could not straighten the thing out in my head, do what I could. If I followed my reason it seemed I should not know which way to go. So I began to hunt for my own track among the stones and along the ledges of rock where I thought I had been—not a mark could I find.

Then I said to myself, although the sun gave me the lie, "Surely if I go to that cliff-top I shall look down right on to the camping-place." I went there and looked down into a great, wide, wild valley I had never seen before—it looked as if no man had ever seen it—I hated the sight of it. I turned back, walked over the crest of the hill and found another ravine. I gazed down; all was still and hot. I could not recognize a single feature of it, certainly it was not the valley we had camped in.

I now began to be really frightened, and with little faith began to turn more towards the sun, but did not know whether to turn my steps north or south—whatever I did the sun always seemed in the wrong place. I crossed a valley, walked over a hill, and came to another ravine very like the last; no, that was not it.

Then I thought to myself I must move no more; I must stay here till they come to look for me. I felt in my pockets, counted my cartridges, and calculated how many shots I dare fire as signal shots. I must fire some at once, as the caravan would be well on its way. I had also a policeman's whistle, my knife, and a pouch of tobacco. I realized if I was not found I must kill meat and drink blood, and that I must keep ammunition for the night, as there was not a single tree big enough to climb into. I fired five shots, counting sixty between each so that they might sound regular, with an interval long enough but not too long to catch the ear of any-one listening for another shot. Our rule was that all signal shots were to be replied to by shots from our men—the camel men carried rifles and carbines. I listened for answering shots; it was all silent in that parched land bristling with the leafless thorns. Well, if my shots were ever to be heard it was now, so I fired two more—deathly silence after the echoes had died away. How I cursed my folly in not telling any one I was going out of camp; as far as I could recollect not a soul had seen me go. My wife was in her tent, hers being the last to come down; the boys were singing and bending over their loads, camels, and tent pegs.

It was my practice to go ahead of the caravan; they would, if they thought at all, think I was in front; my boys, my syce and pony would, when the caravan began to move, go hurrying after me on the line of the day's march, as they had often done before; and if during the day I was missed, no one would guess I had been so stupid as not to start from the camping-place at all.

If they went in search of me it was at least even chances against their going all the way back to the camping-place, and if they did I was not there.

I sat down and blew my whistle continuously for about half an hour, and then got into a state of imbecile terror. The more I thought of it, the poorer seemed my chances of being found that day. It was hot, there was thirst and, worse, there was the night ahead of me. I yelled till I could yell no longer, and my throat became dry and hoarse. Then I tried to remember a method I had read of in some excellent book, like *Galton's Art of Travel*, for finding your way when you were lost. I could remember you had to blaze a tree, and then walk north, south, east, and west so many paces in each direction from your base and blaze trees or make marks at all these points, and then start from them again, and thus keep on enlarging the circle till it intersected your own track or that of your party or some recognizable objects, but the thing swum in my head and the idea of carrying it out in that network of ravines seemed absolutely as idiotic as I had become myself, however simple it might be when mounted on a good horse in a level country. Had there been the possibility of finding water, a recognizable mountain within a hundred miles, or had I even had plenty of ammunition, I do not think I should have got into such a state of terror. After three hours of whistling whilst perspiring with funk, I heard far away in the distance what I thought was possibly a human voice. I again whistled and yelled, but heard nothing more for some time, and then I heard the distant cry again, and determined to fire a shot pointing my rifle in that direction. After this there seemed to be a long and awful silence, and then to my delight I heard that it *was* a cry quite distinctly, but some miles off, and I fired another shot and the cry came again. I continued shouting and whistling, but neither my shouts nor my whistles were ever heard by my shikaris till they got on to a ridge about a mile off; and so I was delivered from my place of torment. It was humiliating to discover myself, after a quick march of about two miles, on the track of the caravan, and I reached my pony after having been lost rather less than five hours.

Really I think my deliverance was fortunate, and it was due to my wife. Our caravan of camels spread over about half a mile. After it had started and the last camel had filed out of the deserted zariba, she had mounted her pony and brought up the rear, expecting that I was far ahead with my boys. After an hour or so she cantered up the line and ahead of the leading camels to overtake me and ride with me. After leaving the camels she came upon my pony and two shikaris hurrying along. She asked where I was; they replied that they supposed somewhere on in front. This did not satisfy her, and she went back and examined the camel men as to when I had last been seen after breaking up camp, but no one had seen me; she then reported this to my shikaris, who were alarmed and immediately set back at a run and started on their search from the old camping-place, each taking different directions and shouting as they went along the ridges. Only one of my shots had been heard, and none of my cries or whistling. A curious thing is that I got so mixed up, that all that day and the next it seemed to me that we were travelling in quite the wrong direction, and to this moment I still cannot get rid of the impression that for two days we were looping back from the general direction of our march. In those five hours I endured all the sensations of overwhelming desolation and fear which have been so often described, and I have known nothing like it in its paralysing effect on mind and senses. It has taught me never to trust alone to the fallible instincts of direction which white men possess, and to observe carefully every piece of ground passed over in new country; I make it a rule whenever possible to have a native with me, to keep touch with my pony when I can, and to carry plenty of ammunition. A friend of mine who was a traveller and ex-

plorer of great experience (the late Mr. George
Grey), had a compass let in to the stock of his
rifle, an admirable precaution and one I recommend others to adopt, though I have never
taken the trouble to do it myself. I have
carried compasses and found them, owing to my
own laziness, of little use, for they are of very
slight service unless under constant observation—
a thing that is not easy to secure when tracking
and hunting, and once lost one's faculty for
believing facts and evidence seems injured.
When once anxiety disturbs one's mental balance
there is a risk of underestimating or over-
estimating distances; nothing has led men astray
so much as this. You may remember that some
little way back you passed a peculiar tree or
rock, and think that you can recover your bearings if you can find it; you retrace your steps,
till you think you have gone too far and must
already have passed it: some such mistake is
generally accountable for the beginning of your
troubles.

Even in England you may walk over the very
track you are looking for without recognizing it;
how much more easy it is thus to miss your way
in lands where tracks are slight, or where game
or natives spread the ground with a network of
paths, those who have wandered in such places
know. Some natives have, like cats and dogs
and other animals, a perfect sense of direction.
I once had a Midgan hunter who never was a

moment at fault, even in a dead-level bush country which he had never seen before and which you could not possibly see out of. I remember, when on the march one day, going off with him on fresh lion spoor after he had had a few words of conversation with the headman to this effect : " How far will you march to-day ? " The headman replied, pointing with his hand, " Till the sun is there, and then we camp." That was all. We tracked the lions for five hours with our eyes on the ground, winding about, in and out, backwards and forwards, sometimes straight in one direction, sometimes round in another ; at about 2.30 p.m. we decided to make for camp, as we had, we thought, a great many miles to go (really about fifteen). I had not the least idea in which direction our course would lie, beyond that it would be northerly, but the Midgan just set off at a very fast walk, and after three and a half hours' riding after him on his bee-line, he pointed at the bright green of my Willesden canvas tent shining through the bush, 300 yards straight ahead of us. He had done this in country he had never been in before, without ever halting or swerving.

I have of late years, when in new countries and elsewhere, carried one of Holland & Holland's signal pistols, firing coloured lights (red, blue, white, or green) in my saddle-bag, leaving another in camp. Time after time have I, by this means, discovered the whereabouts of my camp when belated, and not a few white men with me have spent a night in bed instead of in the bush by seeing the rocket light from one of these pistols rush up from camp and burst into red or white stars in the dark sky. If it can be avoided, it is folly even to cross familiar but uninhabited stretches of country alone and without an attendant. I do not think it prudent to ride even across the Athi and Kapiti Plains unaccompanied, though many of us have often done it ; a broken leg, a fall from your horse putting his foot in a hole, or any slight disabling accident is almost a sentence of death. You might lie there for days, unless, what is much the most likely thing, a lion or the hyænas ate you soon after the first sundown. The best thing to do would be, in such circumstances, to fire the grass—a grass fire would give you light, might keep off wild beasts, and possibly attract a search party.

Such a fire, unless the wind was high, would burn slowly and steadily and would not in a night burn out more than a mile or two of the grass near you ; but did such an accident happen in the rains, your chance of seeing sunrise on these particular plains would not be a very grand one. The following hints may possibly be useful for the novice when out alone :—

1. Carry matches, water, chocolate, or other portable food and plenty of ammunition.

2. A compass if properly used is invaluable,

and a signal pistol in a saddle-bag is a most useful accessory.

3. When lost (if after circling to find your track you fail to recognize it or any particular feature in the landscape, or in the bush, such as a rock, a hill, a tree), calculate how far you have come since you lost your way at the very most; mark the place where you are, and make from this point radii of this distance and walk the circle; if your estimate is correct or slightly over, you cannot very well miss reaching some recognizable object.   When in unfamiliar country observe the ground, trees, or bush you pass by, and with equal care notice from observing the sun and wind the various directions you take.   The wind is a much more dependable guide in Africa than in Europe, for there it will blow out of the same quarter for months together.

With blood warm and in action, in the company of others, even in pain and sickness, and in bed, it may be easy to look Death in the face, but alone in the silent wilderness, with no material foe in sight and in perfect health, imagination conjures up the process of dying as an awful thing and Death appears in a most fiendish shape.   Yet Death which delivers us from pain is no enemy.   Death is blamed for all the preceding miseries with which he has nothing to do.

CHAPTER VI

THE LION

THE majority of white people in South Africa, following the example of their ignorant predecessors, call most of the larger wild animals by wrong names. Not content with giving the names of European deer and goats to antelopes (in which respect we have ourselves largely followed their bad example), and calling river-horses sea-cows, zebras quaggas, hares rabbits, and the like, they call a leopard a tiger, a hyæna a wolf, and a cheetah a leopard. They do, however, manage to call a lion a lion.

They must have arrived at this name for a lion by a process of exhaustion ; for when they had named a cheetah a leopard and a leopard a tiger, what wrong name of exaggeration could they bestow on a lion ? . . . They could hardly call him an elephant, or perhaps they perceived they would be hung up when they came to christen the elephant. There is a sort of free masonry among scientific people, and one of the rules of the brotherhood appears to be to give such Latin or other names to every beast which crawls, climbs, flies, walks, or swims that the wretched millions not admitted to their secrets should not be able to guess what they are talking about. A greater discouragement to general information and interest in natural science does not exist than this, and in my humble opinion no greater service to the study of birds, beasts, fishes, insects, and flowers could be rendered by the learned than in adopting the practice of giving an English equivalent of the names they invent for all created things, so that their books might be " understanded of the common people."

Even the name Lion does not please our scientific friends ; *Leo* is not enough for them, *Felis leo* it has to be ; so that if we attempt to be accurate by their standard we should always say Cat-Lion to distinguish him from all the Dog-Lions, of which there are none. There are cat-lions, there are only cat-tigers, cat-leopards, cat-servals, and so on down to the cat - cats. With the scientific, cats come before dogs ; they are placed at the head of all the carnivora, because they are the highest organized, and have more brain power than the rest; it is therefore useless your discussing with them whether the cat or any cat is really cleverer than the dog or any dog.

The cat has been put first, the only point which ever gave them any difficulty to decide was whether cat or monkey was the cleverer or more highly organized. Here I think the

man in the street will approve of their decision
that the monkey " has it." Had it not been
settled thus, man would now be in a parlous state
in view of the present theories of evolution.
When the learned call a class of animals " Carnivora " they do not mean that the word should
mean quite what it does mean, they do not
always mean that when they say an animal is a
" Flesh-eater " that it really eats flesh, because
they say it in Latin, and you need not be pedantic
about truth or accuracy when you use a dead
language ; this is how the vegetarian bear and
the seals and otters are called carnivora. They
also turn some of the flesh-eaters out of the flesh-
eater family — these inclusions and exclusions
which appear arbitrary to the ignorant amongst
us are not so really, but because the poor
creature has got something the matter with its eye-
holes, teeth, toes, or auditory bullæ. However,
it is enough that for us, Cats are the first family in
the order of Carnivora, and lions are placed at
the top of the lot.

Our Cat-Lion, in adult age, varies considerably
in size. So many are killed by regular hunters
and settlers which are never measured, not to
mention the innumerable ones slain by natives,
that it is impossible to say to how large a stature
the lion attains.

Fortunately for us we can obtain an approxi-
mate idea of their limits of stature, owing to the
trouble which some hunters, like Mr. F. C. Selous,

Mr. F. V. Kirby, and others, have taken to measure and even to weigh their lions and to record carefully these observations. From an examination of recorded measurements there appears to be little difference in the size of fine typical specimens of African and Asiatic lions. In Africa I incline to think that the lions of Tunisia, Algeria, and Morocco attain (or attained) in those colder countries a greater size than those of the Sudan and Central Africa, and that they again tend to be larger in the temperate climes of South Africa. The lions of North Africa fifty years ago were certainly enormous, if not always in height, generally in weight, for they lived almost entirely in many districts on the Arab flocks, and a mutton-fed lion got very fat indeed.

The cold and even wintry climates of the plateaux of the north and south of the African continent account in some measure for the greater proportion of heavy - maned lions that were found in these regions. South of the Vaal and north of the Sahara, the lion may be considered as approaching extinction. It is true, a few still survive in isolated localities, such as the forest regions of the province of Constantine and perhaps eastward into Tunisia, and in some parts of Morocco as well as in German West Africa and the Kalahari. Lions approaching 600 lb. in weight were formerly shot south of the Vaal, and exceeding this weight in Algeria if otherwise credible persons are to be believed. Undoubtedly in some districts of Africa there is a greater proportion of big-maned lions than in others ; but wherever lions are present in numbers, fine black and fine tawny-maned lions have been obtained. For instance, in British East Africa there are much better manes to be frequently seen in such districts as the Uasin Gishu plateau and the Sotik, than, say, on the Athi Plains or in the low countries east of Simba. Yet in every district where lions abound, fine-maned lions are to be found. In thick bush and long grass countries, lions are supposed to have less mane than in more open regions, the idea being that their manes get dragged out and thinned by thorns and brambles, or that the lions scratch out their manes to clear themselves from grass or other seeds.

What gives colour to this theory is the fact that in their lairs considerable quantities of hair, thus combed out, is often to be seen. There may be something in this, but I can certainly vouch for the fact of big-maned lions being found in very thick bush and grass countries, and I incline to think that age and climate have much to do with the production of a fine mane, also that, as among men, some lions of the same family are more hairy than others. In horses, dogs, cats, sheep, and many other animals may be found, in the same distinct breed, a great variation in the thickness, texture, and length of coat—some families of the same breed being more hirsute than others.

In an article on the Mufumbiro Mountains, by Captain E. M. Jack, R.E., which appeared in the *Journal of the Royal Geographical Society*, June 1913, the writer alludes to his experiences with the Anglo-German-Belgian Boundary Commission, and remarks, *à propos* of lions : " Lions were plentiful in the Ruchuru Valley and in Ruanda. Seven were shot by members of the British section and four by those of the German. A lioness shot by a German officer had a mane, a rather unusual occurrence, I believe."

Formerly I used to regard the retention of the spots on a lion, which are so prominent on cubs, as an indication of youthfulness, but I have altered my opinion, as I have never shot a lion, however old, that had not these spots plainly visible, especially along the lower edge of the flanks, where the main colouring of the skin merges into the cream colour of the belly, as well as on the legs. Occasionally slight bars or faint stripes, discernible in cubs, are visible on adults and are to be looked for on the legs. Spots are said to be more distinct on lionesses than on lions. From the instances of longevity in zoological gardens and menageries, the lion may be said to have a life which extends to over thirty years and even to forty.

I have heard well-informed persons, and even hunters, allege that there are different and

distinct varieties of lions. They divide them
into black, grey, and yellow or tawny. Natives
in some lands have the same notion—for instance,
the Arabs of Algeria, who class lions as either
el adra, *el asfar*, or *el zarzouri*.[1] The Boers
distinguish two varieties, the black-maned kind
(*Zwart-voorlijf*) and the yellow-maned kind
(*Geel-voorlijf*).

There is no foundation at all for this superstition, for in the same family you may have a
yellow, a grey, and a black-maned lion. I have
helped to kill two lions side by side the same
morning and on the same spot, evidently brothers,
the one grey with a black mane, the other yellow
with a tawny mane ; when first I saw them
they were walking together in the company of
a light-coloured lioness which escaped. But it
seems difficult to explode this kind of idea, and
the latest one has been to divide lions into bush
and plain lions, which is not worth discussing.

Even the learned among naturalists appear
to lose their mental equilibrium when they get
on to their hobbies of protective colouring and
the like. A very eminent authority lately declared that because lions are tawny they
probably originally lived in sandy and desert
places ; he might just as well say that rhinos
once lived in Coal Measures because they are
black, or that some of the baboons once sat on
the Mediterranean because they are blue behind.

[1] Black, tawny, or grey.

Lions have, however, wandered into the desert where there is game, and some may dwell there and become lighter in colour.

Why should lions want to live in sandy and desert places ? They want to live where there is bush, and grass, and shade, and plenty to eat. The only lions which live on bare sand flats and which walk about in the Sahara are those which prowl about on the canvases of artists at the annual exhibitions of pictures. In an article by a good sportsman, in the *Nineteenth Century* in 1895, appears this curious passage, which sounds like the sixteenth century : " The natives told us that the colour of the skin of both rhinoceros and lion varies with the colour of the soil. Our own short experience quite bore this out, the lions killed on dark soil having a much bluer tinge than those which we had secured on red ground." I wish he had given us some particulars of the red rhinos. What is true is that any animal, including elephants, which either roll or dust themselves in red soil, or beasts which wallow in red mud, *mirabile dictu,* take a reddish tinge. I have seen elephants as red as a brick church—protective colouring again, of course.

In 1909 I several times discussed with Colonel Roosevelt the fascinating subject of protective coloration, and expressed to him my view that our home scientists were making themselves ridiculous by the lengths they went in describing Nature's concealing coloration. Since then Colonel Roosevelt has written by far the best treatise I have ever come across on this question (vide *Bulletin of the American Museum of Natural History*, vol. xxx. art. viii. pp. 119–23, August 1911).

The theorists had till then pushed their doctrine so far as to declare that the coloration of animals made wholly for obliteration, concealment, and protection, and had nothing to do with nuptial dress, advertisement, mimicry, or anything else. Colonel Roosevelt's triumphant exposure of this nonsense delighted my heart, as well as his extraordinarily clever manner in " nailing to the counter " their false descriptions in writing and illustration. Over and over again he takes their preposterous theory and blows it to smithereens with common sense. He quotes from one of these : " The crow's rainbow sheens, so little thought of as concealers, turn him into such true distance colours as he sits on the nest as to rank him at this moment almost with the grouse for indistinguishability," and points out that there is no more chance for his argument than that a coal scuttle planted in the middle of a green lawn is inconspicuous, and shows that there is nowhere and no time when the crow is anything but conspicuous. The idea that *all* animals that prey or are ever preyed upon are under certain normal circumstances obliterative is entirely erroneous.

COLONEL ROOSEVELT KILLING HIS FIRST LION.

To face p. 96.

" There is no conceivable color or combination of colors which may not under some exceptional circumstances be concealing," says Colonel Roosevelt. A British Grenadier in a red coat and a bearskin hat might find himself in some fight in a village surrounded for a moment by red and black objects—red petticoats and black skirts on a wash-line, for instance—which would make his coloration scheme protective. Colonel Roosevelt's conclusions are numerous and well worth study.   The fact is, that no universal law can be laid down.

There is a *tendency* for certain general types of coloration to be found among all the birds and mammals affected by the same physical conditions.   Birds and creatures of the treetops have lighter, brighter, and more varied coloration than those dwelling in more sombre and uniform surroundings near the ground and beneath forest trees.   There is a *tendency* for arctic and alpine animals to be light coloured[1] and often white, for desert birds and animals to have very pale tints, and so on, but the exceptions are numerous; *e.g.* how about the musk-ox, the raven, and the wolverine in the arctic regions, or the cock ostrich and black-and-white chat in the desert ?

There are certain birds and mammals whose coloration is unquestionably concealing, *e.g.* night hawks and grouse.

[1] Where reference is made to Colonel Roosevelt's remarks the American spelling of colour is retained.

Many birds and mammals are advertisingly colored, and often their coloration tends to reveal them to their foes. In many cases the male is advertised and the female concealed by its color, or *vice versa*.

" The species of birds and mammals with a complete obliterative or concealing or protective coloration are few in number compared to those which possess (either all the time, or part of the time, or in one sex for all the time or part of the time) a conspicuous or revealing or advertising coloration, and to those in which the coloration is neither especially advertising nor especially concealing."

I possess no recent printed records of the size of lions, but think an examination of such would show that there is no very great variation in their stature in different regions. It must be remembered, however, that a very small percentage of colonists or residents ever trouble themselves much about measuring their game. I do not suppose 2 per cent. of lions killed even by sportsmen are measured for height, and not 2 per thousand are weighed. I confess to have been too lazy to take this trouble myself, and have never been keen about record-hunting. Any ordinary sportsman should be satisfied with a fine typical specimen of the variety of game he is in search of, and there is no credit in obtaining " a record " through wholesale and persistent slaughter. I knew of one man, I am glad to say

not an Englishman, who killed in one place
some ninety-four Soemerring gazelle and left a
plain covered with his rotting carcasses, not to
mention cripples, without getting a record head.
At that time, a few days north of that place,
I could wander literally among the same kind
of antelope, passing them at times, when they
were grazing, within 10 or 12 yards, and they
have but lifted their heads and gazed at me
with their great black eyes without moving
a leg, and resumed feeding as soon as I had
gone by. Some hideous work has been done in
the name of sport. It is a most legitimate
ambition to secure the very finest specimen you
can for your collection, and the man who refrains
from shooting till he finds a specimen which
satisfies his desires is not only a legitimate
record-hunter but probably the very best of
sportsmen. The publication of records has done
good and harm, for whilst there is no doubt that
it has taught many shooting men what animals
alone are worthy of their attention, it has also
been an incentive to others to continual shooting
in order to get up on the list. There is little
doubt that finer specimens of most beasts have
been and are still secured by men who are as
indifferent to, as they are ignorant about, any
published measurements.

It is impossible to fix how big the largest lion
is. This, however, can be said, that if you run the
tape over a lion lying dead on the ground as he

fell, without " pulling him out," he is a very
long one if he measures over 10 feet from the tip
of his nose to the tip of his brush.[1] In this over-
all measurement the tail counts for much, and a
short-bodied lion may have a long tail and a long-
bodied one a short tail. I have shot three or four
lions about 9 feet 4 inches measured thus, but
none longer. Lord Wolverton's measurement
of a Somali lion, 10 feet 7 inches, is very startling,
but with the aid of a little imagination it is
possible to conceive of a lion even longer. A
pegged skin measurement is not much to go on
unless average width is fairly taken into account,
and there has been no undue stretching. You
can without much manipulation make the skin
2 feet longer than when it was on the body.
A lion 3 feet 7 inches high is a very tall one,
though, I believe, 4 feet has been recorded, and
one whose arm girths 19 inches is a very strong
one, and one that weighs over 400 lb. is a very
heavy one. In fact, if you kill a lion weighing
twice the weight of a good Scotch stag he should
be a fairly fine one, yet some are said to have
weighed as much as three such stags, viz. over
40 stone.

A lioness over 9 feet in length is a very long
one, over 3 feet 3 inches high a tall one, and

---

[1] I have a note of the measurement of an Algerian lion, but
unfortunately cannot quote my authority. It was as follows:
from the tip of the nose to the root of the tail, 2·50 metres; length
of tail, 75 cm. (total length, 10 feet 7¾ inches); height behind
from foot to the top of quarters, 95 cm., or about 3 feet 1⅜ inches.

over 300 lb. in weight a very heavy one. Tigers do not run to any greater sizes, though many have been shot over 10 feet in length, and a very few over 3 feet 6 inches in height, and very few indeed over 500 lb. in weight. The lion's skull is on the average longer than the tiger's, but the skulls in average breadth are about equal. When this has been said, there is not much to choose in point of average size between adult lions and tigers.

The skull of the lion can be distinguished from that of the tiger by the fact that the posterior processes of the nasal bones do not or only just extend as far as the frontal processes of the maxillæ, and that the distance between the anterior parietal suture and the post orbital process is comparatively short, so that the lion's skull may be described as short-waisted as compared with the long-waisted skull of the tiger (Sclater).

Some of the best authorities state that females preponderate largely over males. I have little doubt that this alleged disparity in numbers between lions and lionesses is the result of better observation and inquiry than my own.[1] I can only say that of the scores of lions I have seen I should estimate only one in seven or eight to have been a lioness—this may be pure chance. I am under the impression that two lions at least are shot for every lioness,

[1] *Vide* Major Stevenson-Hamilton's Notes, p. 115.

but then most sportsmen when encountering
several lions would probably shoot at the largest.
Firms like the Boma Trading Co., and Messrs.
Newland & Tarlton, at Nairobi, through whose
hands pass hundreds of lion skins annually,
could give good evidence upon this point.

The generally accepted theory is that a lion,
like a bishop, must be the husband of one wife. I
am not sure about this, for a lion is sometimes
seen in the company of several ladies, and a lady
in the company of several gentlemen, which latter
fact might be considered to argue for a theory of
polyandry. Where lions are not very numerous,
probably they are more frequently found in
pairs, or a lion, lioness, and one or two cubs.
I have seen real, or grass, widow lionesses with
one or more cubs. It is not uncommon to see a
lion, a lioness with two young lions, and one or
two cubs in a family party; and several times I
have come across two old lions and a lioness
living and hunting together. I really do not
know exactly what to make out of their marital
relations, but there is no doubt that a lion often
evinces quite the proper amount of faithfulness
and affection for the particular lady of his choice
for the time being, and will hunt for her and
the young family. The lioness is credited with
even greater devotion to her spouse, so much
so that many hunters, when they come across
a lion and lioness together, shoot the lioness
first, on the assumption that if you kill the lion

the lioness will charge straight and at once, whereas if you shoot the lioness the lion will probably stand by and, before making off, stop to smell the lioness, and when he has satisfied himself that there is not much use in staying any longer he may " clear."

The only personal experience that I can call to mind affecting this question is the following : I once tracked up to a lion and a lioness in Somali bush country; when; after an hour's fast walk on their spoor, I first caught sight of them they were going along freely, apparently quite unconscious that their steps were being dogged. The lioness was leading, and the lion about 5 yards behind. I ran forward in a line parallel with them until I was a little ahead, and I pulled up opposite a narrow glade in the bush which they must cross in full view of me ; there they came, crossing my front at about 60 yards, slouching along with lowered heads; the lioness passed and then the lion was passing. I fired at his shoulder and hit him high in the ribs; he immediately sat up like a gigantic dog begging, but made the ground shake with his rage. I at once opened my gun (a heavy 10-bore shot-and-ball gun) to reload the empty chamber—a precaution worth taking with a double-barrelled weapon whenever possible, so as to secure having two barrels ready in case of trouble. Whilst I was reloading, with an eye on the wounded lion, my shikari at my elbow said, " Look at the other one ! " and there to my surprise, close at my right hand, was the lioness, with her eyes fixed on me with a most dreadfully intent expression and her tail absolutely vertical and as stiff as a poker. I hesitated for a moment as to which to shoot at, but the lion was up and turning towards me, and I gave him the right barrel, only hitting him in the forearm. Luckily, as I thought on subsequent reflection, the great bang of the 10-bore and belch of blue smoke were too much for his fair lady's nerves, for at this shot she bolted, and I wanted my second barrel for the lion, who came straight for me at a shambling gallop— though crippled, so that he lurched as he came, he was determined to get home. At very close range I dropped him dead with a bullet fair between his eyes. It seems to me possible that with a modern rifle with less noise and no smoke this lioness would not have been scared, as she undoubtedly was by the loud report of a big gun in the silent jungle with a heavy charge of black powder. A Somali lion is often so accustomed to the yells of men and to being pelted with stones and firebrands in his nightly raids into native karias that he will take but little notice of the mere noise and flash of firearms. At night at any rate, lions will return to a bait or to your camp time after time after they have been fired at. The foregoing is only a slight indication of what the conduct of an unwounded lioness is likely to be when her mate is attacked.

As to the behaviour of lionesses with cubs, nothing is certain. I have seen a lioness allow her cubs to go away while she skulked behind ; I have fled on my horse from an angry lioness which I had done nothing to provoke, and whose black-maned mate stared stolidly at me with an expression of indifference on his countenance, a sort of savage query in his eyes as to what all the grunting and fury on the part of his lady was about. The following instance, I think, is characteristic of the way in which a lioness will stick to her baby :—One morning my wife, my daughter, and my neighbour, Mr. H. D. Hill, were out riding in British East Africa, when I viewed the finest lioness I ever saw (I was riding about a mile to the right of the rest of the party); she was walking sedately along, followed by a single and tiny little cub. I waved a signal to Hill and the ladies, and she detected the movement from 500 yards away — till then I do not think she had seen me. She immediately popped into a large bush, very thick and about 15 yards square, which spread across a small dry-stream bed, the banks of which were a few feet high. Here she took such complete cover both from sight and from the danger of being shot by a chance ball, that nothing we could do would dislodge her. In turn we tried galloping past, shouting insults at her, firing volleys into every part of the bush ; only once did she ever show herself, when she dashed out for one second at Hill with a savage grunt. He was close to her, and his horse swung and his ball fell short. This was the only attempt she made to bluff us, she had not the least intention of coming into the open or of deserting her infant, and the rest of the day she never so much as growled or snarled once. The siege went on, and all attempts to drive or tempt her out having failed, we fired the dry grass around the bush as a last resource. The fire licked up all round the bush, and flames and smoke swept over it, but never shook her resolution even when they scorched the green leaves above her hiding-place. After hours of exertion, with ammunition nearly exhausted, we gave it up, completely defeated.

I do not think any one could possibly have got this lioness without crawling up the bottom of the furrow—a performance quite beyond our courage. I felt so much admiration for her devotion to the little cub and for the wisdom of her tactics, that my desire to slay the murdering old thing was cooled as I pictured in my mind the tiny creature sheltering in there by its mighty mother.

The period of gestation is about fifteen weeks; the cubs (two to four) are said to be always born with their eyes open. In Central and East Africa I think two litters a year not at all uncommon. In South Africa this is less frequent, and the cubs are born as a rule in the summer between November and March.[1]

Finally, as to the vitality of lions, let me warn the reader against an allegation that appears in some of the best works on the mammals of Africa, viz. that the lion is " not tenacious of life, and is easily killed as compared with the larger antelopes." The lion is a cat and has all the vitality of the cats. I have seen them get away with the most awful wounds and drilled with bullets. I have put into a lion, at from 60 to 20 yards range, six 10-bore bullets solid soft-lead and hollow-point, two 500 solid soft-lead bullets, and two ·256 bluff-point Mannlicher bullets before he would lie down, and finished him finally, after one of my gun-bearers had loosed off one or more Snider bullets into his body, with a shot in the neck. The only possible foundation for the idea that the lion is more easily killed than an antelope is that he is as a rule tackled at much closer quarters than an antelope, gets the full force of the bullet, and possibly that greater pains are taken to aim at the vital spots in a dangerous animal.

The reader is referred to page 214, where he will find a good illustration of the vitality of a fighting lion tackled by good and experienced shots.

[1] *Vide* Major J. Stevenson-Hamilton's Notes, pp. 116 to 120. What he states may be taken as the latest and most authoritative information on this point. See also Mr. A. L. Butler's Notes, p. 137.

Mr. Rainsbeck in his *Land of the Lion*
gives examples of what lionesses can do—and he
considers a lioness at least 100 per cent. more
dangerous than a lion.

One is a case that occurred near Donya
Sabuk, in the bend of the Athi River, when two
men galloped a lioness and lost her in shortish
grass and approached too near to look for her.
In an instant she was on them, carrying Mr.
G. from his pony and biting him through and
through the thigh. Then like a flash turned
on Mr. L., whom she dashed down with a claw
wound across the face which destroyed one eye
and cut through the nose. As she stood on the
unfortunate L., mauling his shoulder, Mr. G.
crawled up, wounded as he was, and blew her
brains out. Mr. L. died a few days afterwards.

Mr. Rainsbeck makes a rather dangerous
statement when he declares : " Nineteen times
out of twenty, however, a lion comes slowly
when he charges." I have seen a good many
charges, but all have been terrific. He adds :
" He sometimes stands for a moment before
finally closing." This may be the experience
of others, it is not mine, but I have no doubt
the statement can be supported and I certainly
believe it possible. I do not accept all Mr.
Rainsbeck says as gospel, as, for instance, when
he declares the Indian lion to be maneless, for
I have seen lions, killed in India, with quite fair
manes.

CHAPTER VII

THE DISTRIBUTION OF LIONS

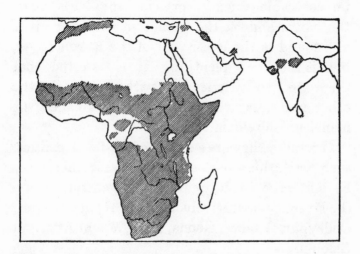

THE above sketch map attempts to indicate the distribution of lions throughout the world in recent times, and the only areas in which lions are likely to be found now.

It is difficult to find reliable information as to the present distribution of the lion in Arabia, Persia, and towards the Afghan and Indian frontiers, and also as to some parts of Asia Minor. They certainly still exist in Mesopotamia between the lower Tigris and Euphrates, and are said to be numerous in certain districts of Southern Persia.

I find in my notes on the fauna of Asia

Minor, made during a journey in that country in 1891, the following :—

The lion is no longer found in Asia Minor, but it exists in Mesopotamia and Arabistan, between Poelis, west of Aleppo, and Deyr, and in the Euphrates Valley, where it frequents the impenetrable thickets growing in places along the banks and on the islands in the river ; it is also found in the lower part of the Karun River, but is nowhere plentiful. It is asserted that there are two varieties, one with a mane and the other maneless ; the latter variety is called the maneless Babylonian lion.

In India they are surviving in a few localities, such as Kathiawar in small numbers ; there may be odd ones in Rajputana. A generation ago they were comparatively common about Jodhpur, Oodeypur, Gwalior, Goona, Kota, Mount Abu, and Lalolpur.

In 1830 lions were common near Ahmedabad. The last lion to be killed in the Allahabad country is said to have been killed in 1864.

Formerly lions ranged as far west as Greece and Roumania, and at some remote period were distributed over Italy, France, Spain, Germany, and the British Isles. Such remains of *Felis leo* as have been found in Pleistocene formations of the temperate regions of the Old World indicate animals of a larger size than any surviving in the warmer regions where the lion is now found.

In North Africa lions up to the time when

firearms were freely distributed, and even up to the occupation of Algeria by the French, were very numerous in suitable countries. By the middle of the last century their numbers had been greatly diminished. This decrease was largely due to the high price placed on their heads by the Turkish Government in the Barbary States, a policy continued on a smaller scale by the French in the countries conquered by France.[1] Their favourite haunts, within the memory of man, were the forest-clad hills and mountains between the Ouarsenis on the west, the Pic de Taza on the east, the Djebel Ennedate on the south, and the plain of the Chelif to the north. There were also many lions among the forests and wooded hills of the province of Constantine and eastwards into Tunisia and south into the Aures; the cedar forests of Chelia and neighbouring mountains harboured lions down to about 1884. In addition to the native lions of Algeria, " Berranis," *i.e.* " foreign wandering lions " as the Arabs called them, wandered over the country from Dir Guezoul, Djebel Dira, and Zakkar. When first I knew Algeria there were occasional lions in the Dju Djura, the Aures, along the Tunisian border countries, and throughout the region from La Calle to Soukarras. A European whose name and nationality has slipped my

---

[1] Two tribes which devoted themselves to lion-hunting, viz. the Ouled Meloul and the Ouled Cessi, were freed under the Turks from all taxation, and were paid liberally for skins.

memory, though I think he was a Russian hunter, killed a large number of lions between 1880 and 1895 in the neighbourhood of Soukarras. During the nineties I myself hunted almost the whole range of the Atlas from the Oued Chair in the west to beyond Tamerza in Tunisia, and visited likely mountains to the north of the Aures, like Chelia, and never came across a single lion track. The last lions I heard of in Algeria were some distance to the north of Bordj bou Arreredj, in 1899. Since 1900 I have hardly hunted at all in Algeria. The Algerian lions preyed on flocks and herds, and it was no uncommon thing for them to become man-eaters of the boldest and most accomplished kind ; Gérard, who himself slew some thirty lions between 1848 and 1856, relates how one lion exterminated the population of a *douar* (the tribal assembly of tents), killing forty Arabs, and he calculated that one single tribe, of about one hundred tents, suffered in losses of horses, cattle, and sheep, from the depredations of lions, an amount equal to a tax of £8400 a year. Between 1873 and 1883, that is, in the decade immediately preceding my first visit to Algiers, the Government return of lions killed (the Government grant being then 50 francs a skin) was as follows :—

Algeria .	.	.	.	29
Constantine	.	.	.	173
Oran .	.	.	.	0
			Total .	202

AN ALGERIAN LION.

[Photograph by Fernandus, formerly of Biskra.

To face p. 112.

The following figures show how the numbers diminished :—

	Number Killed.
1878	29
1879	22
1880	16
1881	6
1882	4
1883	3
1884	1

The following dates mark approximately the retreat of the lion from existence in South Africa :—

1707. Lions not uncommon near Cape Town.

1801. Lions still met with in the Karoo and Witenhage.

1842. Last lion south of the Orange River (recorded by Hall and quoted by Sclater) killed near Commetjes Post.

1865. Last lion killed in Natal by General Bisset (Sclater).

1898 and 1898. Lions killed at Springs (near Johannesburg) and Heidleburg.

1903. Occasional lions still seen and killed in the Transvaal outside the Game Reserves, and common within the Reserve and in Portuguese East Africa. During my residence in the Barberton District, 1903 to 1905, I several times saw lion spoor in the neighbourhood of Kaapmuiden and

Komati Poort, and noted the following occurrences outside the Reserve in the Barberton District :—

1904. Seven lions seen at Malelane.

1 lion killed by Palns near Kaapmuiden.

Several seen at Hector Spruit.

Others seen on the railway at various times by engine-drivers between Crocodile Poort and Komati Poort.

One seen near Low's Creek. (This name is Leuw's Creek, *i.e.* Lion's Creek—a lion-haunted valley when the Dutch first arrived.)

1905. Three seen at Mananga.

Others reported between Hector Spruit and Mananga.

1913. The lion is still found in Zululand, the Eastern Transvaal, German South-West Africa, the Kalahari, Rhodesia, and Portuguese East Africa.

Major J. Stevenson-Hamilton, writing to me from the Sabi Game Reserve, Komatipoort, on the 1st July 1913, gives the following interesting information :—

" As regards your questions, I cannot give you any reliable statistics as to the number of lions accounted for in the Transvaal outside the Game Reserves, as there are none available. I should say, however, that the number killed does not exceed half a dozen annually, and I doubt if it even reaches this figure. Within the Reserves the total accounted for to end of the present month since 1903 is 190, the totals being as follows : 1903, 6 ; 1904, 2 ; 1905, 10 ; 1906, 13 ; 1907, 13 ; 1908, 21 ; 1909, 25 ; 1910, 21 ; 1911, 32 ; 1912, 36 ; 1913, 11 (to end of May). Sexes about equal in numbers.

" Up to 1905 we administered only about one-fourth of the area now under control, which partly accounts for the divergence of the present figures. Naturally, as time went on, haunts became better known, and the staff more efficient. Numbers are probably a little less than they were a few years ago, but there is no danger of extermination.

" Outside the Reserves I should say the animals were probably slightly increasing where the big game is not poached, as they are seldom shot ; elsewhere where game is decreasing the lions take toll of donkeys and cattle, and are now and then shot or poisoned ; but, take it all round, the majority of the public have, as they say themselves, ' not lost any lions.'

" I have never weighed a big lion, I am sorry to say. The *average* full-grown lion here in the Eastern Transvaal measures about 9 feet 6 inches over all before skinning, and the lioness about 12 inches less. They are of all sorts, black-maned and yellow-maned, and entirely or almost entirely maneless in the same localities, though I think they tend to be fuller maned on the whole in the south. The same as to body colour, from extremely light to very swarthy. Full-grown lionesses of over three or four years old sometimes show quite distinct spots, and others have no vestige of them. I have noticed the same divergence in young animals under a year old from the same troop. I have the skins of three cubs of six months old from the same litter, two males and a female, and none are quite similar either in hue or spotting.

"I have never seen or been apprised of any cases of albinism here, though some lionesses are certainly extremely light in hue, nor have I heard of any cases of melanism, though I have shot one or two extremely swarthy males.

"Now as to the extremely important and much-vexed question of breeding of lions, I hope you won't take anything amiss I may say, should it disagree with your own great experience, but this is a matter I have been studying very carefully on the spot for some eight years, and I find my views are largely in disagreement with many of those popularly held.

"In 1905 Dr. Gunning of the Pretoria Museum was intending to give a lecture on the subject of periods of gestation in wild animals, and, talking the matter over with him, I determined to ascertain as far as possible whether lions (and larger carnivora generally) bred annually in a wild state as they do in captivity. It had always seemed to me that, seeing that these

animals produce three or four in a litter, of which
two generally reach maturity, in the course of
ages, before firearms and even man at all came
on the scene, they would have increased out of
all proportion to the herbivora which have only
one offspring annually if they bred as often as the
latter. This was of course only a rough specula-
tion, because on reflection it is obvious that when
they had reached a certain point there would be
nothing more to eat for the large majority of
lions, and so they would mostly die of starvation
or fail to mature, and Nature would have had
to make a practically fresh start from the few
remains of the herbivores and carnivores. But
I think from deduction of what little we know
we may assume that such cataclysms have not
been the general case at least.

" Again, lions (and leopards and chitas) are
not independent within a few months of birth, as
are the herbivorous ungulates generally. They
are, on the contrary, very weak and helpless for
a long time, and even after they have acquired
strength they accompany their mothers in hunting
and act under their mother's tuition. I do not think
Nature allows the mother to renew maternity
until her last offspring are quite independent of
her, and in the case of lions this certainly does
not occur until their large canines are well
developed and they have learned to kill large
game unassisted. I don't think eighteen months
is too long a time to allow. We can't judge in

the least by the methods of captivity, where conditions are absolutely opposed to the wild state, and where the future of the young ones is amply provided for even if they are not taken from their mother as soon as weaned, in which case, of course, she would be quite ready for a new family.

" Since 1905 I have had so far as possible all the full-grown lionesses killed opened, and carefully examined, and the result has been that only comparatively a small minority have been found either to be in milk or to have embryos inside. Some of the negative cases when killed had been accompanied by male lions and by one or more big cubs of at least a year old, so that if their habit had been to breed annually they would have shown it by the embryo, or, by containing milk, have proved that they probably had small cubs secreted somewhere.

" I am therefore very strongly of the opinion, which I base both on what seems to me to be most in accordance with natural design for due balance, and on the practical study I have given to the matter, that lions, here at all events, not only do not breed twice annually, but seldom oftener than once biennially (excepting only in the case of a lioness which has lost all her cubs of the last litter).

" I am aware that this is opposed to the general belief, which I take it is largely based on observations in captivity, but on the other hand I doubt

if many hunters have had the opportunities of
going into the matter under natural conditions
as I have, or have kept records in the same way.

"You will find some statistics on the subject
in my book, *Animal Life in Africa*, as well as some
other points about lions as they have seemed to
me here.

"Now as regards size of litters, the average
here certainly seems to be three or four, judging
from embryos taken from lionesses, but two have
not been infrequent. Latterly, however, that is
in the last three or four years, four seems to be
a common number; whether this is chance or
whether the extremely easy manner in which
lions can now get food—since the game has
increased so largely and their own numbers have
been artificially kept down—has increased breeding power, I cannot say, but this much is certain,
that whereas seven or eight years ago lionesses
with cubs seldom were found with more than two
and more often one only, now it is not uncommon
to see four well-grown cubs with a single lioness.
This seems a very interesting illustration of the
way in which Nature, as it were, gets her own back
on man. We destroy the enemies of the herbivora as much as we can and leave the latter
alone. Nature, by providing a correspondingly
increased food supply for the lions, sees to it that
a larger proportion of the offspring shall survive
than is the case under absolutely natural conditions !

" A side result has been that native stock (and our own) in the game country is perfectly safe, and such a thing as a raid, except very occasionally by a more or less decrepit animal, is almost unheard of. On the other hand, outside the Game Reserve in the Zoutspansberg district for instance, and just outside our western boundary, stock-killing is quite common, because there is hardly anything bigger than reedbuck, and lions which have strayed a bit out of their usual beat find themselves driven by hunger.

" The most usual time for cubs of lions to be born here is during July and August (especially August), but they are certainly born all through the months from March to November in lesser numbers, and I have records of young cubs seen, or lionesses containing embryos which would have been born soon, for every month in the year.

" I have so far no reports of more than four cubs to a litter."

In North-East Africa there are lions to the north of the Bogos country, and here and there right through Erithrea to the Tackazi and westwards, and south into the Sudan. In the Blue Nile districts, as well as on both sides of the White Nile, lions are plentiful enough, and are to be met with in almost all districts of the Sudan. In Abyssinia they must be getting very scarce, but on all sides of the Ethiopian plateau

they generally abound; through the Galla
countries and to the south they are said to be
practically ubiquitous, till you reach those parts
of South Africa where the white settlers have
wiped them out. Of West Africa I know nothing
personally, and cannot state where they are most
numerous or where they are becoming scarce.

SOMALILAND

In 1905 Colonel Swayne, the British Commissioner for the British Somali Coast Protectorate, estimated the number of lions then
in British Somaliland at about three thousand.
Since 1905 the British Government have abandoned most of our possessions and fellow-subjects
to our victorious enemy, the Mullah, and the
country to anarchy. The Somalis have acquired
firearms, and probably the lions within this area
and outside have been greatly reduced, not only
directly but by the wholesale slaughter of the
game on which the lions subsisted.

THE SUDAN

Mr. A. L. Butler, the Superintendent of the
Sudan Government Game Department, has most
kindly furnished me with the following information. These notes are of so much interest that
with his permission I publish them in full.

NOTES ON THE LION IN THE SUDAN

By A. L. Butler, Esq.

1. *Present Distribution*

For the past twelve years—since 1901—I have kept a map to show the distribution of the lion in the Sudan, and marked on it every place where they have been shot or met with as far as my information goes. The following notes, taken from this map, may therefore be considered a fairly reliable sketch of the range of the species in this part of Africa :—

Prince Henry of Liechtenstein has told me that in 1880 he came on the tracks of a lion in a *wadi* about half-way between Berber and Suakin (about 19° N. Latitude and 36° E. Longitude). The killing of one west of and near the Nile, north of Berber (18° North), is, I believe, within the memory of old native inhabitants. But at the present day the northern limit of the lion's range seems to be about midway between 16° and 17° North Latitude. South of this, lions occur on the Atbara from near Goz Regeb to Gallabat, at Filik (about 50 miles north of Kassala), on the Khor Baraka, the Gash, the Setit, and the Bahr el Salaam. In this district they are most numerous on the Atbara near Mogatta, and on the Setit, and appear to have increased in numbers within the last twelve years.

On the Blue Nile and its tributaries, the Rahad and the Dinder, they are fairly plentiful south of

Sennar, within a short distance of which place
they still put in an occasional appearance.
They are perhaps most abundant on the Rahad,
from which river they sometimes wander north-
wards to El Fou and Gedaref, where one was
shot in September 1906.

On the Blue Nile they are most plentiful on
the west bank.

On the White Nile they range north to
Jebelein, where there are generally a few about
near the hill, and I have once known of tracks
being found north of Kosti. Mr. Seton-Karr
met with four males together on the west bank
near Renk this year, and shot all of them.
South of this they are fairly common between
Renk, Jebel Ahmed Aga, and Kaka. Between
Kaka and Taufikia they are scarce, owing to
the openness of the country and the abundance
of Shilluk villages. Near Tonga round Lake No,
and along the Bahr el Ghazal they are numerous.
They are particularly abundant on the Zeraf
River (where four were killed simultaneously by
a volley from a steamer last year !), and also
occur on the Sobat, Pibor, and Akobo.

On the Bahr el Jebel they are absent in the
" Sudd " region between Lake No and Shambe,
but doubtless inhabit the dry country at the
back of these vast swamps. South of Shambe
they occur on both banks of the Nile to Rejaf,
and range across the country eastwards to the
Pibor and Akobo.

West of the Upper Nile the lion ranges practically all over the Bahr el Ghazal Province, and is found in the vicinity of nearly all the numerous small rivers (which are too numerous to mention in detail), and north all along the Bahr el Arab. I find my map is fairly well sprinkled with record marks between 25° and 31° East, and 5° and 10° North.

Farther north again their extension into Kordofan lies mainly between 28° and 30° East, to a little above the 11th parallel.

Very considerably north of this, however, lions occur again sparingly out west in the Wadi Milh (about 15° North and 28° 30' East), and I have heard of tracks being met with near El Ein, just south of the 16th parallel. This brings their northward range west of the Nile nearly into line with their northern limit in the Eastern Sudan, as previously described. A cub of these desert-dwelling lions was brought to me three years ago from the Wadi Milh, and its remarkably pale coloration is referred to elsewhere in these notes.

To sum up, while west of the Nile the range of the lion lies mainly south of 10° North Latitude, on the east it is well distributed for some 5° farther north.

2. *Variations in Type, etc.*

Sudan lions generally have very poor manes. In the east of the country (Atbara, Setit, Rahad,

Dinder, etc.—thorny bush-country) the mane
is usually not more than a scanty ruff, and nearly
always of a yellow colour. Lions that I have
seen shot in the Bahr el Ghazal Province near
Wau were much the same in general appearance.
I have seen some moderately well-maned skins
from the Blue Nile.[1] There is often more
development of the mane, with a mixture of
black in it, on the open grass country near Lake
No, on the Bahr el Ghazal, Bahr el Arab, and
Zeraf, but here again a meagre yellow ruff only
is not infrequent. I have only once, several
years ago, seen a lion with a really fine mane in
the Sudan, and this, curiously enough, was on
the Rahad River. This was a regular picture-
book lion, by far the finest I have ever seen,
with a really magnificent mane of a blackish
or very dark colour, and a dark greyish body.
Though I was able to watch him through glasses
on two evenings in succession I could not get a
satisfactory shot at him. I do not think this
splendid beast was ever shot. Certainly, no
skin with such a mane has since come through
Khartoum.

Cubs appear, as a rule, to be darkest farther
south. I have seen them from the neighbour-

[1] In *African Nature Notes*, p. 76, Mr. Selous figures three lions
showing different developments of mane.

His No. 3 would best represent the majority of Sudan lions
I have seen. The best manes I have seen might be as well
developed as in his No. 1, or perhaps a little less so. The big
black-maned lion I saw on the Rahad *looked* quite as good as
No. 2.

hood of Lado with a dorsal line and the spots
almost black.

Very different was a cub brought in to me
three years ago from Wadi Milh (15° North,
28° 30' East), in Western Kordofan. This was
a remarkably pale whitish, sandy, or isabelline
colour, with the back of the ears and tail tuft
grey instead of black, and with only faint traces
of spots. Its appearance suggested that the
desert-dwelling lions of this region are coloured
much like the smaller mammals (hares, mice, etc.)
of sandy deserts. I should very much like to
see an adult lion from this locality.

On the whole, I do not think I could recognize
with any degree of certainty the locality of a
lion from its appearance, unless perhaps it was
a cub from the south or a lion from the north-
western desert.

I have never known of a case of albinism or
melanism.

3. *The Food of Lions*

The staple food of the lion varies a good deal
in different districts, according to the nature of
the country and the game found in it. You
say that your experience was that round Lake
No they fed principally on white-eared cob.
This is quite correct, and applies equally to the
Zeraf River and the Bahr el Ghazal. I would
add that the victims seem to be almost always

adult males. They scatter about more than the females, and are therefore doubtless more easy to stalk singly.

Where cattle, goats, and sheep are plentiful, as on the Atbara, Rahad, Blue Nile, and lower White Nile, they are preyed on a good deal. These domestic animals are generally shut up in zaribas by night, but lions which have taken to cattle-lifting become pretty bold in attacking them by day. At one time and another, a good many losses have been sustained among Government transport bulls in the Bahr el Ghazal. In the Eastern Sudan camels frequently fall victims. In 1900 two lions killed a camel on a path near the village of Sofi on the Atbara, and remained on it, holding up all-comers, until the late Colonel Collinson, then Governor of the Kassala Province, happened to ride up on a favourite shooting pony and promptly shot them both from the saddle. I have twice known of a camel being killed near El Fou, between the Blue Nile and Gedaref, one of them by a single lion. On one occasion an Arab came to me on the Atbara and said his camel had just been killed by a lion. His story was that he had dismounted for a rest and had gone to sleep under the shade of a heglik tree, while his camel remained close by him, browsing on the branches. He was suddenly awakened by an outbreak of roaring and grunting (presumably the camel's), and found his camel and a large lion struggling on the ground within a few yards of him. Having no weapon but a sword, he wisely took to his heels and left the camel to its fate. I had not time to visit the spot.

On the Atbara and Setit ariel and wart-hog are a common prey. On the Dinder ariel and reedbuck appear to be most often killed, but young buffaloes, roan antelope, waterbuck, wart-hog, and even giraffes all pay a regular toll.

I do not think old buffaloes are often attacked, but on one occasion, on the Dinder, a sportsman following up a badly wounded bull came upon a terrific struggle going on between it and three male lions. This soon ended in the buffalo succumbing. Three quick and accurate shots laid the attackers dead round their victim— making a remarkable bag !

Full-grown giraffes, in spite of their great size and strength, are killed occasionally, pro-bably more than one lion attacking at the same time. I have known of several cases. Quite recently an officer at Roseires wrote to me, to report having finished off an old cow giraffe which had been recently mauled about the head and neck by a lion and blinded in one eye. When found, the animal had wandered out on to some rocks extending into the Blue Nile, among which it had fallen and was unable to rise.

Major Stevenson-Hamilton records that in eight years he has only known of one authenti-cated case of a giraffe being killed by lions in the Transvaal Game Reserves. This was an old bull, in the killing of which four or five lions took part. The greater frequency of such occurrences in the Sudan is doubtless due to the much greater abundance of giraffes, which are extremely plentiful in many districts.

Kudu are a frequent and favourite prey, and I think a considerable proportion of them are killed by lions, their bush-frequenting habits doubtless constantly leading them into ambush. Porcupines are occasionally tackled, presumably by inexperienced or very hungry lions, unable to find other prey. It is not uncommon to find their quills embedded deeply in a lion's paws or body, and I have heard of a lion dying from the effect of quills stuck in the throat. A complete list of the animals I have known killed by lions would be : Camel, horse, donkey, cattle, sheep, goats, giraffe, buffalo (young), eland, kudu, waterbuck, roan, white-eared cob, ariel, reedbuck, bushbuck, wart-hog, tiang, hartebeest, and porcupine. Probably a good many smaller animals are eaten and no trace left of them.

I have heard of young elephants being killed, but cannot vouch for this personally.

4. *Man-Eating Lions*

I have known of a few instances of natives being killed and eaten by lions, but African natives, with more courage than those of India, are generally prompt in combining to exact vengeance for this offence, and a lion is seldom allowed to live to develop regular man-eating habits. (It was probably owing to the immunity from retaliation which they enjoyed after first commencing to attack *Indian* coolies that the famous man-eaters of Tsavo became such a terrible scourge in the district. I fancy most African tribes would have managed to get rid of these murderers at the start of their career.)

In August last year, three lions which used to hunt in company killed six men near Lau, in the Bahr el Ghazal. One of them was then surrounded and killed with spears, and the survivors apparently left the neighbourhood.

In 1906 (I think it was) a party of Mohammedan blacks from west of the Sudan, pilgrims, travelling by slow stages to Massawa on their way to Mecca, arrived one evening at Mogatta on the Atbara. The road near the river is bordered on both sides by dense thickets of " Kitr " thorn, and as the party was passing through this a lion sprang into their midst, seized an unfortunate boy of fifteen or sixteen, and in spite of the shouts of the others, dragged him away into the bush. Terrified at this incident, the rest of the little party descended to the river, and camped for the night in an old and dilapidated zariba near the water's edge. During the night, which was a dark one, their frail shelter was besieged by three lions. Eventually one broke into the zariba and dragged off a

second victim—this time a man. For a minute
or two his cries for help were heard receding
into the darkness, and then all was silence.
Next morning two constables from the small
police post at Mogatta followed the trail of the
dragged body into the " Kitr " bush, and found,
about a quarter of a mile away, one of the unfortunate man's feet. The tracks showed that
a lion and two lionesses had taken part in
devouring the victim. The following day I
arrived at the place with my cousin, Mr. H.
Boughton Leigh, and we devoted a few days to
trying to bring the murderers to account.

A bullock tied up in the neighbourhood was
killed, and Mr. Boughton Leigh shot a big lion
over it the next night, but whether this was one
of the offenders it was impossible to say, as there
appeared to be several lions about. I never,
however, heard of a man being attacked there
since.

Twice I have known of natives being seized
at night and dragged a short distance, but
dropped again on their companions rushing
out with shouts and firesticks. Both these
men, though badly bitten, subsequently recovered. I saw one of these men—a Hanran
on the Setit—a few days later, and he must
have had a wonderful escape, as he had been
seized by the neck, in which the great canine
teeth had made terrible wounds, without,
however, touching the spine or carotid

artery.   I doubt if a European would have recovered.

5. *Number of Lions killed in the Sudan by Holders of Game Licence since* 1900

1901	.	.	.	. 23
1902	.	.	.	. 25
1903	.	.	.	. 12
1904	.	.	.	. 23
1905	.	.	.	. 33
1906	.	.	.	. 27
1907	.	.	.	. 32
1908	.	.	.	. 26
1909	.	.	.	. 18
1910	.	.	.	. 17
1911	.	.	.	. 27
1912	.	.	.	. 25 (not yet complete)

288

Allowing a small percentage for returns not received, the number of lions bagged by European sportsmen in the Sudan during the last twelve years would be over three hundred.   It is my belief that a larger proportion of lions are lost wounded than of any other animal, owing to the temptation to take any long chance they offer, to their powers of concealing themselves when wounded, and to hesitation in following them up in thick covert.   If it were to include wounded

lions which have died without being recovered,
I should be inclined to raise this total to five
hundred.[1] This does not include lions killed by
natives. This is an uncertain quantity, and may
not be very large, but I think a good many cubs
are annually killed with spears in one part of
the country and another. Also numerous cubs
are picked up and brought in alive to different
stations.

6. *Lion-Hunting Accidents*

During the last twelve years there has only
been one fatal lion-hunting accident to a
European. This was the case of Mr. Salmon,
an engineer of the Steamers Department, who
wounded a lion from a steamer, and then landed
and followed it up in grass. He was charged
suddenly, and his rifle missed fire. Salmon was
a powerful and resolute man, and in the struggle
on the ground which ensued he succeeded in
opening a small pocket-knife. With great coolness he tried to stab the lion through the eye
to the brain with the tiny blade, and actually
succeeded in driving it home between the ball of
the eye and the socket, but only with the result
that the lion immediately seized and broke his
right arm. It was shot on him by one of his
men a few seconds later, but Salmon succumbed
soon after to his injuries.

[1] A man once told me he had wounded nine lions, but never
got one !

The only other accident to a European which I can remember occurred to Mr. Wyndham Jones, an official of the Works Department, who fired at and mortally wounded a lion from the back of a mule. The animal charged home; the terrified mule got foul of a thorn bush, and the sportsman was seized by the knee and dragged to the ground, the dying animal fortunately then leaving him. He was, however, severely injured.

7. *Measurements and Weight*

On these points I have little information to give. I have never had an opportunity of weighing a lion. Several average full-grown males which I have measured were all about the same size, 8 feet 9 inches to 8 feet 10 inches. Lionesses, 7 feet 8 inches to 8 feet. (This is absolutely straight measurement between a spear driven into the ground at the animal's nose and another at the tip of the *bone* of the tail.)[1] I have seen one or two lions which, I am sure, would have been a good deal larger.

Of height at shoulder I can find no exact notes. I should say it was much less than has often been recorded from measurements taken without the animal's weight on the shoulder-blades and feet.

[1] The measurements given on page 100 are taken by running the tape along a lion from the tip of his nose to the tip of his brush—which method gives greater length than the one employed by Mr. A. L. Butler.

8. *Breeding—Number of Young—Mortality among Cubs*

In all the cases known to me in which newly-born or very young lion cubs have been found they have been two or three in number—perhaps more frequently three.

I do not think there is any particular breeding season. Cubs seem to be born at any time of the year. I have often had cubs of very different ages and sizes offered to me during the same month.

I am convinced that there is a very high mortality among lion cubs in a wild state, and I doubt if half of them live through their first year. Certainly it is far commoner to see a lioness accompanied by one or two large cubs than by three.

Considering the short period of gestation (Major Stevenson-Hamilton gives it as about one hundred and eight days), the number of cubs produced at a birth, and the few enemies they have to contend with except man, lions might reasonably be expected to be much more numerous than they are, and this heavy death-rate among the cubs is probably Nature's way of keeping their increase within limits.

Over and over again I have lost apparently strong and healthy wild-born cubs in captivity without being able to ascertain the cause of death. They begin by showing a staggering gait and a loss of power in the limbs, which grows worse until it renders them quite helpless, and ends in their dying practically paralysed. I have never known one recover after developing these symptoms. Only a few days ago I had to destroy a lioness cub about seven and a half months old which had become quite helpless. Up to a short time before, she had been a healthy and lively cub. She had never been shut up and had had plenty of exercise. A most thorough post-mortem examination (kindly conducted for me by Dr. Chalmers of the Gordon College Wellcome Research Laboratories, assisted by two other medical men and an Army Veterinary officer) showed no obvious cause of the animal's condition. She was free from visible internal parasites, and showed no signs of " rickets." I am waiting with interest the result of microscopic examination of various blood slides and other material taken from her.[1] At the same time, I have a very fine young lion of about a year old (at the stage in which the first canine teeth are still retained by the side of the growing permanent ones) which is beginning to lose the power of its legs in just the same manner. I believe that these cubs would have gone the same way in a wild state. Major Stevenson-Hamilton, who, with a great experience, also recognizes this heavy mortality among cubs, mentions the finding of two young lions between

[1] This examination gave no positive results, and had not solved the mystery.

six and twelve months old, "dead, with no obvious cause to account for their demise."

I have never come across any evidence of lionesses breeding twice in the same year, and I believe that more than this interval usually takes place between the birth of one litter and the arrival of the next. A lioness will often be accompanied by one or two cubs apparently at least a year old, but I have only once heard of one being seen followed by cubs of different ages. In this case she had with her three very small cubs and one which was probably well over a year old—presumably the sole survivor of her last litter.

9. *Some General Notes on Habits, etc.*

I have never heard of lions in the Sudan associating in the large troops which have so often been met with in other parts of Africa. Once I was told of seven being seen together, but this included some half-grown young ones. Five and four together have been met with quite frequently, all adult. I once saw three old males and a lioness walk down to a pool on the Rahad to drink, in single file, with the lioness bringing up the rear. Three or four old males often join forces and hunt together—the partnership probably terminating in the members going off singly " to seek their loves again ! "

So much has been written about the habits

of the lion by many more competent writers, that my own limited experience is mainly confirmative of observations already recorded, and adds little that is new. A most excellent account of the animal's life history is given in Major Stevenson-Hamilton's *Animal Life in Africa*.

In the Sudan any sort of country seems to suit them, excepting, I think, heavy forest in the south. On the Atbara and Setit the dense and extensive thickets of " Kitr " thorn (*Acacia mellifera*) afford them a safe covert. The " Kitr " growth is open enough beneath to allow them to pass under the lateral spread of the branches, which unite to form an impenetrable barbed entanglement 3 feet above the ground. *Zizyphus mucronata*, a bushy thorn tree which grows near the rivers, and carries green leaf throughout the year, forms a dense and dark canopy under which lions are fond of tunnelling and lying up. Reed beds and islands of high grass in dry river beds are favourite haunts. On open plains they will lie up for the day under any meagre shade-tree. They are partial to the neighbourhood of small rocky hills, or " jebels," though I have never seen them actually on them.

As a rule, lions are seldom found far from water, but in Western Kordofan they sometimes occur at a great distance from it. Natives assure me that these desert-dwelling lions obtain sufficient moisture by eating water-melons. This is probably true. Jackals certainly do so, and in case of necessity desert Arabs can subsist on water-melons for a considerable time.

It is well known that lions are good swimmers, and will take to deep water readily. I remember two being shot swimming across the Zeraf River.

Where they have not been made shy by persecution, lions do a good deal of their hunting by day. I have known them kill at almost any hour between sunrise and sunset. On one occasion, when Mr. G. Blaine and I were travelling in the Bahr et Ghazal Province, three male lions attacked and killed one of our donkeys close to camp in the early afternoon. Blaine hurried to the spot and knocked over all three of them, but, while he was finishing off the third, one of the first two recovered and managed to escape.

Lions often show great boldness in attacking cattle and goats in the daytime, and in returning to their kills again shortly after being disturbed.

I have heard them roaring up to 8.30 in the morning and as early as four o'clock in the evening, but never in the middle of the day. They are much more silent at some times than at others. On a recent trip up the Dinder my wife and I only heard one lion roaring, though we saw two, and fresh tracks were abundant.

In quiet localities they will often come down to river pools to drink before sunset, and on the Rahad or Dinder there is always a chance of getting a daylight shot by watching a pool, where their tracks are numerous, from four o'clock till dark.

I have previously mentioned a very fine black-maned lion which I once saw on the Rahad. There were two small pools in the dry river bed, close under the same bank, and about 200 yards apart. From the tracks it was evident that a very big lion was in the habit of drinking at either of these, approaching them across the sandy river bed from the opposite bank, on which he apparently lay up. I waited by one of these pools in the evening, and just before sunset the lion came down to the other. It was a long shot to take, and I preferred the chance of his coming to the pool I was at on another occasion, so I contented myself with watching him through glasses. The grand old fellow lapped away for a long time, and then, having drunk his fill, lay down at the water's edge, scooped up a great mound of wet sand with his paws, and then lay with his great fore-arms round this and his chin resting on it, enjoying the contact with the cool, moist surface. The next evening I waited by that pool. He came again, but to *the other*, and again he made his mound of wet sand and lay embracing it, after drinking. Again I refrained from shooting in the hope of getting a close and certain shot on the following night. But on the third evening he happened to be on my bank instead of his

SOUTH AFRICAN LIONS.

[*Harris's, South Africa.*

To face p. 140.

own. Apparently he winded me, as he roared behind me several times and then drew off. At any rate, he did not appear again that evening or the next, and I had to leave the place without seeing him again. I fancy his method of making a mound of wet sand to cool himself against was an individual habit. I have never known another lion do the same.

Lions are very observant, and I think they often locate a carcass by watching the descent of the vultures. I once witnessed an undoubted case of this. I had killed a roan antelope on very open country, and when about a mile from the spot I turned round to watch the vultures dropping down to feast on the remains. Two lions were slouching across the open plain, making a bee-line for the carcass. A premature attempt of mine to stalk them caused them to retreat. They were approaching down wind, and as the carcass had not been there an hour before, they could not have known of its position except by the vultures. I have seen jackals follow the birds in the same way.

A full-fed lion is sometimes a heavy sleeper, and I have heard of them being almost trodden on unexpectedly. In 1902 a steamer stopped in the Bahr el Ghazal to cut firewood, and for two or three hours the whole vicinity was thoroughly disturbed by the sound of axes and the noise made by the men. Presently an old black came up to Mr. G. B. Middleton, the engineer of the boat, and said there was a lion lying asleep at the foot of an ant-hill close by. Incredulous at first, Middleton eventually took a ·303 and went to have a look. There was nothing visible as he approached the ant-hill, and, with a little run to gain impetus, he scrambled on to the top of it, by no means noiselessly. To his astonishment, a full-grown lion lay fast asleep just below him. He lost no time in putting a bullet through its head, killing it instantaneously.

I am by no means certain that lionesses always show the desperate valour in defending their cubs which is generally attributed to them. I have never come on newly-born cubs myself, but I have repeatedly known them picked up and carried off by practically unarmed natives, without the mother showing up at all. Nor have I heard of any exciting adventure attending the carrying off of cubs.

Little more than a month ago, a Russian officer who was shooting on the Dinder fired at, and slightly wounded, a lioness which emerged from some high grass, and on receiving the shot promptly bolted into it again. There was a certain amount of blood, and he cautiously entered the high grass in search of the wounded beast. There was a growl close in front of him, and a sudden rush through the grass, as the lioness—made off! Then, almost at his feet, he noticed two tiny cubs lying side by side. These he picked up, and succeeded in keeping alive, subsequently sending them in to me as a present. They were the smallest cubs I have ever received. Here was a case of a lioness, hurt and furious, concealed in thick grass with her enemy within springing distance, not only retreating, but abandoning her cubs without an effort to defend them.

Major Stevenson-Hamilton records a case in which a lioness, aware that her three cubs were being carried off, contented herself with protesting from covert. This frightened the captors into dropping the little things on the road. During the night the lioness removed one of them, but was apparently too nervous to return for the other two, which were found next day where they had been left, dying from the exposure to the cold of a frosty night.

Possibly in many cases the mother is away foraging when her offspring are found.

But that both lions and lionesses vary immensely in courage and temperament there can be no doubt. Personally, I think a lioness is generally the nastier tempered and more dangerous of the two, and the more prompt to charge. I have heard of a lioness, unwounded, and not in milk, which had been marked into a small patch of grass, charging boldly out directly this was approached, and being killed as she came.[1]

---

[1] Probably she was aware that she had been seen, and conscious that her patch of covert was insufficiently large to afford a good chance of escape.

When a lioness makes up her mind to charge, she comes in with extraordinary rapidity. I have only been charged once, and when I was expecting it, but I quite underestimated the pace at which the animal would come. This was near Filik, north of Kassala. Mr. Boughton Leigh, who was with me, had killed a lion at a water hole the night before, and wounded a lioness. There was a fair amount of blood on her tracks, which we followed next morning into some long grass. Presently I saw her about 40 yards ahead, crouching very flat, with her eyes fixed on me. I was carrying a double 10-bore, but, thinking my Mauser would be more accurate and just as effective for a forehead shot, I called a man up with it. Taking the smaller rifle from him, I placed the 10-bore, cocked, on the ground by my side, and sent him back. The lioness remained perfectly motionless, except for the twitching of her black tail tassel—a dangerous sign. I imagined that if I failed to kill her and she came for me I should have ample time to pick up the 10-bore and get in a couple of shots with it. A few stems of grass waving in the breeze in front of her face were rather baulking, but I took a steady shot at her forehead, and thought I was dead on. The response was instantaneous. She launched herself forward absolutely on the shot, and was half-way to me before I realized that she had started, and within a couple of strides as I got

my hand on the grip of the second rifle. I am
not sure that I should have had time to use it,
but at that moment my cousin fired from some
little distance on my right and cut her spine
well forward with a ·450 bullet, bringing her
down, completely paralysed, just in front of me.
At the pace at which she was moving, it was an
extremely good shot. The shot of the night
before had only inflicted a nasty flesh wound
under the chest, while my inaccurate shot with
the Mauser had only furrowed her cheek. I
should ask for a hundred yards in which to get
in two aimed shots on another occasion!

When burnt out of a patch of grass, lions
will often wait until the last moment, when the
flames are almost up to the end to which they
have retreated, before breaking covert.

The following is one of the most remarkable
lion-shooting incidents I have known of, though
the chief interest of the story was provided
by a leopard. A lioness had killed a bullock on
the Blue Nile in the daytime, and an Austrian
sportsman who was on the spot concealed himself close to the dead beast. Presently the
lioness approached, creeping cautiously towards
her kill. Just as she reached it the watcher
became aware of a leopard also approaching
stealthily from the other side, the two animals
being only a few feet apart, and unaware of each
other's presence. At this point the sportsman
shot the lioness through the heart; she gave a

convulsive spring forward and rolled over dead, colliding violently with the leopard as she did so. With a perfect explosion of snarls, the leopard vanished into the grass, and was seen no more, but by the body of the dead lioness *it left a tiny cub, expelled prematurely in its sudden terror.* The result of this shot was, therefore, one lioness, one leopard (spirit specimen)! I saw both trophies.

It sometimes happens that an enthusiastic desire to encounter *Felis leo* evaporates when the longed-for meeting at last occurs. I remember a sportsman who went up the Nile with the slaying of a lion as his dearest ambition. Before starting, he questioned me as to all the most likely places to find one, and the advantages and disadvantages of every possible shot was discussed at length. I was away when he returned, and a glance at a " game return " of waterbuck and white-eared cob showed that my friend's ambition had not been realized. But he left me a note to let me know how he had got on. " We saw two lions," it ran, " but unfortunately they were engaged in eating a white-eared cob, *and were in no mood to be deranged.*"

THE DESTRUCTIVENESS OF LIONS

The destructive powers of lions can scarcely be exaggerated when they depend, as they did in North Africa, almost entirely on domestic flocks and herds. In one district of British East Africa where game swarms, and where the same lion will kill every night practically the whole year round, I have made a rough calculation as to what lions kill there in a year. My immediate neighbours and I killed more than forty lions in eighteen months, and if these only kill one beast a day on three hundred days in the year, this alone means 12,000 head of zebras and antelopes killed in twelve months. Then for every lion killed we have seen two or three others, and had news of many more; but assuming that we have killed half the lions, and that this region had been the feeding-ground for only eighty lions, that would mean 24,000 head of game to feed them. Again, a lion is often not satisfied with one kill, and often cripples and mortally wounds several zebra in his rush into a herd. In Somaliland a single lion is often not satisfied with killing a single camel for his dinner, and will kill two or three; I have seen this myself. A good idea of what man-eating lions can do will be found truthfully described in Colonel Patterson's *The Man-Eaters of Tsavo*.

Further instances of the destructiveness of lions will be found on pp. 112, 160, 194 et seq.

CHAPTER VIII

LION CUBS AND TAME LIONS

THERE is an idea that lionesses in their wild
state never produce more than two or three cubs
at a birth. I do not think three cubs at all an
uncommon number to see with a lioness. There
are a number of instances of lionesses in captivity
having given birth to as many as six cubs in a
litter ; it is difficult to believe that no such litters
are ever produced by lionesses in their wild state.
Authorities seem agreed that the mortality
amongst small cubs is great, which accounts for
two or one being the more usual number met
with.[1]

Cubs are born with their eyes open, and are
very easily tamed. I have been in houses where
they were quite at home, playing with people
or dogs, and became quite charming pets ;
though they should never be trusted when they
grow up. I have also undergone some nervous
strain in the company of adult tame lions.
Once when in Abyssinia I strolled in at the

[1] The Arabs in North Africa ascribed the mortality in cubs
to the difficulty of eating during the period of dentition.

Herodotus states lionesses only bring forth one cub, and that
the cub tears its mother's inside with its claws !

gate of M. Ilg's garden at Adis Abeba, to pay my
respects to this great State functionary and his
lady. I was aware he had some tame lions, but
I was not prepared to see them strolling about
on the path I took up to his house, and was
devoutly thankful when I had passed the great
slobbering brutes.

Talking of tame lions, I may mention a curious
sight that was a common one in Algeria in the
nineties, and for aught I know may yet still be.
I wish for a second time to record it, for I have
heard of my story being given in another volume,
as an instance of the credulity or mendacity
of travellers. On the 19th day of October 1892,
my wife and I were driving along the road
between Blidah and the Gorge de la Chifa, in
Algeria ; we were not then as familiar with that
beautiful country as we became afterwards,
and hopes, since smashed to atoms, of killing
lions there were then young and strong, and now
and again I heard of lions as having been seen in
the Dju Djura range. Now as we rolled along
the dusty road I saw a very fine maned lion,
freshly killed, being carried on a donkey which
staggered along under its heavy burden; the
lion's fore-paws scraped the ground on one side
and his massive head hung down in the dust ;
on the off side the tip of his tail trailed from time
to time on the road. An Arab led the donkey,
and two other natives with big sticks in their
hands walked alongside. I stopped our carriage,

jumped out, and ran after this party, calling to them to halt ; they did so, and before I got up to the donkey I asked them where they had killed the lion. "Mackash môt " (Not dead), said one of the Arabs, and then another gave a tug at a stout short bit of rope which was round the lion's neck. To my infinite surprise, the lion scrambled off the donkey and was led towards me.

He was an old, yet fine and healthy specimen, quite blind, having had his sight but not his eyes destroyed, to render him more tractable. I was much interested, and asked what this strange company were doing. I was told that this was a sort of sacred lion they took from place to place, and that everywhere it was in great request for the exorcizing of evil spirits, curing the sick, and for driving away the plague. I give a very good photograph of this same lion, which I met again a year or more afterwards at Biskra, and which I introduced to a photographer, who forthwith had him taken out of the town and then took this portrait of him on the bank of the Oued Biskra.[1] The Arabs believe in people being possessed by evil spirits, and they make out a very good case for their creed.

Probably the treatment by lion is very efficacious in many cases of hysteria, though sometimes a medicine of the mending or ending kind. These lions are taken into the houses and sick-rooms, and their attendance is well paid for.

[1] *Vide* illustration, "An Algerian Lion," p. 112.

A SACRED LION ON DONKEY-BACK.

To face p. 150.

After my wife and I had spent some time examining the lion and his keepers, one of the attendants gave it a whack with his stick, and it turned of its own accord to where the donkey was standing, and scrambled over it, hung itself down at both ends as before, and the donkey bending under its weight trudged bravely forward again.   The lion appeared once more as limp and lifeless as a sack.   I one day met this lion in the corridor of the Hôtel Victoria at Biskra; my little daughter was with me and attempted to pat it, but, as she related afterwards, she did not like it, for when she " stroked it, it snorled and browled so."

I told a Parisian acquaintance of mine of this lion's presence in the town; he forthwith dressed himself in the best French chasseur style, and sallying forth, armed with his shot gun and attended by the photographer, had the lion laid out prostrate in the desert, and then was photographed standing over him in the most splendid pose of a successful hunter.   This photograph gave him immense pleasure, and copies were posted as fast as possible to Paris.

It is extraordinary what a *chasseur enragé* will do.   I know an English M.F.H. who was overheard muttering to himself whilst his hounds were eating their fox after a good run, " Now why the —— can't I do that ? "   I think some Frenchmen in their ardour would have eaten a bit, for most certainly I have observed the

custom amongst them of eating the meat of
any unusual trophy that is shot.   I have known
them have lion and panther cooked to eat,
which seems to me far worse than eating fox;
yet I came across a passage somewhere in Mr.
Selous' writings where he said he had eaten
lion, and that it was quite eatable and something
like veal.   Tastes differ, and some people may
find cat excellent, but the sickly horrible smell
of cat flesh is concentrated in the odour of lion
meat.   I have seen Midgans in Somaliland eat
lion flesh.

I am tempted, à propos of lions as exorcists,
to tell another story, in spite of the risk of having
it set down as a "traveller's tale"; but I am not
without a living and credible witness to vouch
for its truth.   Once when Sir Edmund Loder
and I were travelling in the Tunisian Djereed,
or rather on our way thither, in the desert south
of Nefta, one of our camels, which for several
days had been too sick to carry its load, showed
signs of early dissolution.   At the end of a long
day's march it just dragged itself into camp and
sank on the ground; for several days it had
refused to feed or to be fed.   Sir Edmund and
I inspected it, and agreed that the most merciful
thing would be to shoot it; it would evidently
not rise again.   " I would not give sixpence for
him," was Loder's remark as I turned on my
heel to call an Arab to shoot it.   Our headman
to whom the order was given said, " All right,

but you know the Soufis (he was a Soufi) do not
consider this camel ill but possessed by a devil,
and some of them can drive evil spirits out of
men and beasts." I replied in a somewhat
jeering tone that they had better try their powers
on this subject. He asked me whether we did
not believe in evil spirits, and whether they
were not in our religion. I answered rather
lamely that they were in our Koran, but I did
not think many Christians had much belief in
them. The exorcist-in-chief among our Soufi
followers appeared on the scene and got to
work ; this is exactly how he proceeded : " In
the name of God," he cut a bit off the tip of the
animal's tail so that it bled; he then took a
kous-kous dish, a large wooden platter, turned it
upside down under the camel's nose; on this he
placed a handful or two of black gunpowder. He
then took in one hand a red brand from the
camp fire and in the other a handful of barley,
this last he placed beside the powder. After a
few moments the camel lowered his head and
smelt at the barley, and the Arab at once touched
the powder with the burning stick. " Poof "
went the powder, enveloping the camel's head
in flame and fumes. When the smoke cleared
away you could hardly imagine what a poor, woe-
begone, abject creature our camel was. All
the hair and whiskers were burnt off his head,
face, and lips; he was blackened and without
eye-lashes, and a sorry object indeed.

We went off a little amused at this exhibition of superstition, and rather disgusted, but at all events quite confident that we should not see the camel alive again. What was our astonishment in the morning, as we started at daybreak, to see the possessed one standing with his load, clothed, so to speak, and in his right mind. I do not attempt to explain it, but just state the fact that this camel from that hour, for weeks after, showed no signs of indisposition, mental or physical, but did his daily task and took his nourishment like the best of his companions, and that had it not been for this fumigation he would never have left that camp. Fumigation has, I believe, been for some thousands of years accepted by exorcists as one of the most efficacious treatments for the possessed.

EXORCISING A CAMEL.

To face p. 154.

CHAPTER IX

THE HAUNTS OF LIONS

Lions frequent forest-clad mountains and valleys,
and bush countries; they will lie up under
solitary trees or in single bushes on plains and
open country, or have their lairs in high grass
and reed beds; they are fond of dongas and
dry stream beds, and are as often found in
such places where cover is slight, as in the jungles
on the banks of running rivers and streams;
they make their dens also among rocks and great
boulders on kopjies and hills as well as in caves
and caverns. In the daytime I have seen them
sunning themselves outside cover, on the edge
of bush and on slabs of rock; it is curious that,
in the few lion countries traversed by railways,
they seem particularly fond of lying about on
the permanent way. In the Barberton district
of the Transvaal, when I knew it, lions were not
common and were hardly ever seen, except by
the railway men and engine-drivers, who often
saw them basking on the railway between Kaapmuiden and Komati Poort, whilst on the Uganda
Railway they are constantly seen. Lions seem
particularly fond of walking on man-made paths

of any description, they have a wandering disposition for the most part, and at times cover great distances without halting ; doubtless they find our roads a great convenience, though their presence does not add much to the comfort of the wayfarer on the King's highway. I have traced lions for miles along a railway. In dry seasons and districts they come to the railway to slake their thirst at the pools below the locomotive watering tanks. As many as three lions in a night have been shot by one man out of a machân fixed in the scaffolding of the tanks adjoining the railway station platforms at Simba on the Uganda Railway; and it is by no means rare for a stationmaster and even passengers to see a lion walk through the station on a journey up or down the line in the early hours of the morning before the sun is hot.

Mr. Rainsford gives in an appendix to his book some amusing telegrams received by the Traffic Manager from the Stationmasters on the Uganda Railway. Here are two :—

SIMBA.   17.8.05. 16 hrs.
The Traffic Manager.

Pointsman is surrounded by two lions while returning from distant signal and hence pointsman went on top of telegraph post near water tanks. Train to stop there and take him on train and then proceed. Traffic Manager to please arrange steps.

TSAVO.   20.4.08.   23 hrs. 35 mins.
The Traffic Manager.

2 down driver to enter my yard very cautiously points locked up. No one can get out. Myself Shedman Porters all in office. Lion sitting before office door.

As an illustration of the lion's fondness for the Uganda Railway, the late Mr. Currie when he was Manager of the railway told me he had on his journeys up and down the line (generally seated on the cow-catcher in front of the engine) in less than two years counted over seventy lions on the permanent way.

In the days when lions were numerous in North Africa they hung around the douars, for there alone was food in sufficient quantity for them. In Somaliland at this day, after the rains begin, about April, and the grass of the prairies on the Haud is green, the Somalis move their karias with their camels and sheep to these rich pasture lands; the lions follow them down, for some have discovered that it is easier to prey on domestic animals, and others are attracted by the abundance of game which, like the Somalis, seeks the fresh grass.

An old lion, whose agility is failing, or who from long-enjoyed impunity has developed into a purely "karia lion," becomes entirely dependent on the village communities, or even on a single village. On one occasion, in a part of the waterless Haud where game abounded, I killed one of these lions in a starving condition ; the native population had trekked north a month previously, as the grass was withering. He was gaunt, tucked up, a bag of bones with his skin hanging in folds, his eyes were sunken, but I provided him with one good dinner before he died. On the march, the day of his last repast, I had gone aside late in the afternoon and shot two fine oryx bulls, side by side, for meat, and then had galloped after our caravan, and sent back two camels to where I had left my shikaris skinning them, to cut them up and bring them into camp. My shikaris, having finished their job, met the camels and directed the camel men, who were four or five in number, and armed with carbines, to the place and then hurried after me. When we had pitched camp the camels returned, but without the meat ; they reported that though they arrived at the place a few minutes after the shikaris had left the two dead oryx, they found a very big and vicious lion in possession of the two carcasses, and that he had so terrified them with his voice, gestures, and charges that they dared not dispute the meat with him. The next morning at dawn I made my way to the place, and saw the top of the lion's head and his tail swishing under a little thorn bush, into which he had drawn one of the carcasses. The conduct of this surfeited lion confirms the theory of the magnanimity of lions

after, rather than before, meals. He certainly
behaved in a nasty, selfish way, just before dinner
the night before, but with very great consideration
for me the next morning, with one oryx bull
inside him.

From about 60 yards I fired at the place
where I thought his head was and hit him in
one of the fore-paws, on which he was resting
his chin; he got up and stepped out, making a
noise, but did not attempt to charge, and stood
almost broadside, with his head turned rather
towards me. I hit him with my second barrel
in the ribs; he went slouching off, and I ran after
him, firing a good many shots at him. I was a
little blown in my efforts to get near him, and
though I got up close behind him he only once
faced round and looked somewhat reproachfully
at me, and then trotted on again. I put at least
five 10-bore bullets into him before he lay down
and gave it up. This lion, which had scattered
four or five armed Somalis and made them fly
before him, and which I anticipated would be a
terror, exhibited, I think, the least ferocity of
any I have ever encountered at close quarters.

As far as I know, it is comparatively rare for
lions in British East Africa to prey regularly
on either native villages or flocks and herds. I
attribute this largely to the vast quantity of
game which is there, and to the ease with
which it can be obtained. A lion would be a
very poor one which could not catch a fat zebra,

and were he too old or too feeble to do this, there are so many lions about that he need do no more than attach himself to a party of his kind, or visit the abundant kills.

At the same time, I know from my own experience that it is very unsafe to trust to a mere thorn zariba (or boma, as the zaribas are called in British East Africa) for the protection of cattle or ostriches. Had it not been for the devotion of my neighbours (Messrs. C. and H. D. Hill), who have taken turns on many nights on the roof of my ostrich and cattle sheds, and defended my stock from lions attempting to break in, my losses would have been very serious up to the time when I was able to erect ten-foot high iron sheeted fences. Even after I had an iron and high wired fenced in boma we lost over thirty ostriches in one night, killed by three lions which clawed down the fence. Ostriches penned in bomas appear to be attractive bait. One moonlight night in 1909 my next-door neighbour, Mr. Harold Hill, sat up in a tree in the middle of his thorn ostrich boma expecting the return of some lions which had called on him the previous night; sure enough he was rewarded by the delightful sight of seeing his precious birds being chivied round and round the little enclosure by five lions; as soon as he began to shoot they seem to have gone demented, and they whirled round and round inside the boma, whilst he felt as if he was sitting on the pole of a merry-go-

DEFENDING AN OSTRICH BOMA.

To face p. 160.

round. He had splendid sport and practice at flying lions that night, bagging four of them and, I think, wounding the fifth; several were not gathered till next day, and one lioness at least gave some trouble before she was dispatched. I am not positive that the bag was not five, but I know it was at least four, for he sent four of the skins up to my house, thinking they would help me, as they did, to furnish my new house before Colonel Roosevelt's arrival. In every country where lions are numerous one occasionally becomes a man-eater, but considering the number there are in British East Africa, and the density of the native populations in certain parts, there are remarkably few which get into this nasty habit. No doubt the extraordinary ease with which they can feed themselves, owing to the immense quantity of game, has something to do with this; but I have known places where it would be impossible for game to be more plentiful, yet where lions will occasionally pursue a man on horseback, or follow a man on foot, even in broad daylight.

It is rather an ordeal, at least to me, to walk or ride through certain stretches of lion-haunted grass on the Athi and Kapiti Plains, especially when alone. When in company I have experienced a sense of relief on emerging, for it is easy to ride right on to a lion in these places, and should he be nasty he might easily collar you before you could shoot, and if you are unarmed, as you never should be, and if he gets up only a short distance off, escape on such ground would be impossible, for you could not gallop.

Not so very long ago, one of my nearest neighbours, Mr. Philip Percival, was riding alone through one of these places, not very far from the Kapiti Plains Railway Station, where it was possible, at considerable risk of a cropper, to gallop; he was mounted on a noted old lion-hunting horse belonging to his brother the game ranger, who had accounted for many a lion in his company. This horse is well known to us by the name of " Weary "—having ridden him myself I can vouch for the name being appropriate, for, save in pursuit, or when pursued by lions, he affected the most tired and blasé air imaginable; he was never known, save in the chase, to break voluntarily out of a walk. Percival had in his hand a ·256 Mannlicher rifle and was wending his way homewards over the vast plain, when to his surprise " Weary " began to trot. Trying to account for this quite unprecedented exhibition of vitality, he turned his head to see if there was any after cause—to his horror, he saw a great lion coursing right for him, and drawing on at the awful pace a lion can; at this particular moment the lion was some 40 yards behind, in another second he would be at him—in went the spurs and away " Weary " went, with death at his heels, as he never went before; but the start was not enough, a few moments more and the lion's great head came forging up to " Weary's " quarters. There had been, of course, no chance or time to shoot, and at this instant, in this terrible race for life, it was still impossible, as any one who has tried to fire behind him on a horse extended in a gallop over rough ground knows well enough ; Percival, believing that his last moment had come, sent forth, he declares, the most piercing yell that ever issued from human throat. The lion was so astonished at this very unusual note that he forthwith pulled straight up, and stared with astonishment ; meanwhile, if such fractions of time can be called " whiles " even when they appear eternities, " Weary " was going his best pace, hell for leather, and ere the lion had recovered his surprise had put in a fair distance between himself and his pursuer, perhaps a hundred yards ; then the man-hunt began afresh and the race for life went on ; " Weary " exerted himself to his utmost, the lion began to lose ground, and when the horse had drawn out two or three hundred yards the lion abandoned the chase. Percival reined up and sprang off, with shaking hand and heaving chest, fired a shot or two at his retreating enemy, but did not hit him nor hurry him much in his somewhat leisurely retreat.

How often have I seen Percival among lions with his cool head and steady nerve ! Yet it is said, and I have not heard him deny it, that on getting home he sat down in his house and remained there a solid week, using really shocking expressions; he admitted to me that it was some months before he recovered the slightest desire to see any more lions. No one who has seen him, as I have, since this adventure, crawling into their lairs or rounding them up, would ever guess he had at any time suffered any shock to his nerves.

Mr. Selous says he has seldom known lions attack in this way in the daytime, but gives one or two instances.

There are not a few of the most experienced big game hunters who make the assertion that it is almost unknown for lions to attack in the daytime. This assertion may be found in several recent books where the lion's habits are discussed or described. During my residence in British East Africa, it was by no means uncommon for lions to attack the Indian bullock carts on the road between Machakos and Kapiti Plains Stations by daylight. Probably most of these attacks were between five and eight o'clock in the morning, but I am not sure that some were not as late as ten a.m. Nearly all I heard of were in the neighbourhood of Wami. In June, 1911, a young Dutchman employed by Mr. Russell Bowker on the Guaso Nyero, by name Postma, had arrived one morning at dawn at a little stream known locally as Deep Dale, with his waggon and oxen. He had no sooner let the oxen loose than they were attacked by nine lions. Postma jumped on to the waggon and picked up his ·350 rifle and opened fire on the lions who had at once pulled down and killed one of the front oxen. In less than ten minutes he had fired ten shots and killed seven of the lions (three lions and four lionesses), and had wounded the two others, which, however, escaped. The seven lions lay dead before Postma, the farthest away being only fifteen yards distant from him.

CHAPTER X

THE LION'S VOICE AND THE LION'S EYE

THERE is no sound which issues from the throat of any creature to compare with that of the lion's voice. It has sometimes been likened to the noise ostriches make, and this is true to some extent of the distant roar of the King of Beasts; but heard near at hand, in the dark or in daylight, his roar is a truly terrible and earth-shaking sound. The awful notice to every living beast that their king is walking the silent night to deal out death, whilst it strikes with terror on the ear of every creature of the forest and wilderness, cannot fail to impress the listening man with awe and often with dread. Why do lions roar? Why do they announce their oncoming in the night or their departure, as with bloody lips they leave their horrid work, in the cold dawn? Do they roar after their prey? Do they roar from pangs of ravening hunger, are they challenging or calling or courting or just defying all creation, or is it the outcome of mere love of boastfulness, making all this noise? I do not know. I hear them on dark nights when they are turning the plains into shambles as they

prowl among the whitened skulls left from a
hundred cruel feasts; but I hear them too in
the morning, when the first sunlight is slipping
quietly forward over the hills, and the vultures
are gathering for their turn; more often I hear
them about an hour or so before dawn, when
they have had their fill of flesh. It is noticed
that lions become much more silent in districts
where they are constantly hunted; from what
I have heard from those who first lived near
the Athi and Kapiti Plains, it would seem that
though lions were not so very much more numerous then than at present, they were far more
noisy. Certainly you may now spend several
weeks together there with lions around you and
only hear them two or three times.

Not long ago, Mr. Selous told me that he
considered it a fact that they refrained from
roaring where they were much disturbed. Any
one may hear the noise a lion can make, at feeding
time, in the lion house at the Zoo, yet somehow,
though the air vibrates and the sound comes
thundering out of the depths of their insides,
it gives little sensation compared with that of
standing in the bush on a still night, and not only
hearing, but feeling it close at hand. I have led
my horse in the dusk when light failed too much
to ride among the trees, and heard but the deep
grunt of a lion, perhaps a quarter of a mile away,
and felt it so full of meaning that my blood has
run cold and I have cocked my rifle and tugged

at my horse to hurry him home. The roar proper consists of an ascending scale of half a dozen awfully deep and loud moaning, reverberating roars, ending either with a sigh that makes the air quiver, or low rumbling growls which shake the earth. Until you are familiar with them the mere deep staccato chest grunts of a lion, when you suddenly disturb one or come up with one, are very disconcerting. Whenever you put up a lion at close quarters, even when he means to bolt at once, he generally gives these sharp grunts as he jumps up. A lioness with cubs will stand and grunt at you from a distance, and leopards will make a coughing grunt rather similar to that of a lion which has spotted you ; at least I have several times mistaken the one grunt for the other, which I suppose a better observer would not be likely to do. Near the place where I resided on the Mua Hills, British East Africa, lions may be heard roaring as late as eight or nine o'clock in the morning, but this is rather uncommon.

THE LION'S EYE

It has been said that the lion's eye is not luminous ; I assert it is luminous, even after death, giving forth shining light of pale green and gold, whilst in life it seems to flash forth fire. I have seen photographs of lions taken by flashlight at night where the eyes of a startled

LION ROARING AT DAWN.

To face p. 168.

lion shine like glowing orbs. But I cannot say
that I have ever seen, when gazing at a lion face
to face, even a yard or two off, from the secure
shelter of a zariba, on a dark night, any sign
whatever of light in their eyes ; my own opinion
is that their eyes, like certain other eyes, have
the power, even in dim lights, of collecting and
reflecting concentrated light to a very remarkable degree. That their sight in the dark is
extraordinary has been generally accepted, and
many are the legends founded on their powerful
vision. Talking over the camp fire with my
Arabs one night we were discussing the comparative sight of various animals, and one of
the men said, " You know the result of the trials
of sight made by the Prophet ? " I shook my
head ; he then related this legend :—

" When Mohammed the Prophet had tested
the sight of all living creatures, he found that
Allah had given the best vision to the horse
and to the lion, and that they could see by night
as we see by day and even more distinctly ;
he devised a final test on the blackest night
there ever was, which should decide for ever
between these two, the most wonderful of all
his creatures.

" Having put before them two bowls, one
containing milk with a single white hair in the
milk, and the other containing pitch with a
single black hair in the pitch, he accorded the
first place to the lion ; for whilst the horse picked

the white hair from out the milk, the lion at once took out the black hair from the bowl of pitch."

Lions see exactly what they are doing at night, and the blacker the night the easier they seem to find it to pursue and kill their prey. Horses see extraordinarily well at night, and long ago I learnt from the Arabs that when guarding camp from hyænas or two-legged prowlers of the night, there is no sentinel superior to the horse, nor a better indicator than his head. All is still and dark save the light from the camp fire, which makes the surrounding blackness more impenetrable, and which shines, it may be, but faintly on the forms of the picketed horses. As you sit gazing and listening, you see the horses lift up their heads and remain motionless awhile, you neither hear nor see anything; their heads turn, *they* see something—one of them snorts softly, and you can note that they are following with their eyes an invisible something which approaches; as it draws on, the heads move more perceptibly, and you will know whence it comes and how near it draws on—at the moment you judge best (for the final rush of a lion or hyæna is swift as lightning and very sure) up goes your gun and breaks the silence of the night. One night like this in the Sahara, in a region notorious for camel robbers and horse thieves, I was hidden in the darkness watching my horses thus and aiming at a spot my horse was staring at steadily, when the Arab nearest me said : " Do not fire, it may be one of our own men." We looked round to see if we were all there, and this movement in camp no doubt alarmed the thief, for the men heard some one running away before I fired. By daylight we traced where one of the marauders had crawled up near on his hands and knees and waited, at the very place my horse was staring at ; the tracks of the robber's flight were also plainly visible. In such places as these, it is advisable to have your horse's legs fixed in locked iron shackles, as mine were on this occasion; but though this defeats a thief it does not improve a horse's power of self-defence against wild beasts. I have known a Somali pony tied by the head to a tree keep a lion off with his heels, and to be standing uninjured in the morning in the midst of a well-padded circle of lion tracks.

CHAPTER XI

SOME WAYS OF LIONS

WRITERS of authority declare that lions never climb trees, that they never jump any height, and that they never bound or spring when attacking. Again I say, it is not safe to say that lions *never* do this or that. Lions will at times climb trees, and indeed in one or two regions they are quite addicted to climbing certain forest trees; in a particular one which, owing to the presence of the tsetse fly, has no resident native population, the neighbouring Gallas and Somali gum hunters are the only people to be found there; these go in on foot for the sole purpose of gathering gum. As a rule gum hunters, when away from home, find security at night in the trees; but in Burka it is notorious that they are not safe in ordinary trees, and that many a gum hunter has been taken out of trees by Burka lions.

Two well-informed and truthful Somalis, whom I knew well, thought it a habit peculiar to the lions of Burka, and in a wide and long experience of lions could not cite an instance of climbing lions elsewhere in Somaliland. There

is, however, little reason, given trees proportionate
in size and form, why the biggest of all the cats
should not climb trees like others of this family.
Tigers have been known to climb trees, and
during inundations to swim out and climb on
board a steamer — there is nothing in their
structure generally nor in that of their claws
to prevent their climbing ; yet unless a tree has
large branches and a trunk out of the vertical,
it is rather difficult to picture them getting far
off the ground, though if branches were strong
and numerous it is conceivable that they could
get up a very straight tree. As to their ability
to jump and spring there is no doubt whatever.
They often come into native karias in Somaliland over dense thorn zaribas 10, 12, or even
more feet in height, and not only jump in, but,
incredible as it may seem, will take a fair-sized
camel out. I have never seen it done, but have
seen where they have done it and am certain
they do it. On questioning some Somalis who
showed me a Gadabursi zariba fully 12 feet
high, out of which a lion had taken a camel,
they said the lion seized and dragged the camel
by the neck and swung it on to the fence,
then jumping over he pulled it down on the
other side and trailed it away. But this is not
more remarkable than a story told me by Mr.
James Saunderson, in whose veracity I im-
plicitly believe ; it is one I have often been laughed
at for repeating. I told it to Colonel Roosevelt

in 1909, and he could not resist poking fun at me gently for days after. This is what Saunderson told me :—

One day when he, with a friend, was hunting in Portuguese territory, he shot a young giraffe, and left the carcass out as bait for lion or leopard ; on returning the next day they saw a leopard, and after following it, shot it. On going back to the t ee again, under which they had left the giraffe the previous day, they could see nothing of it until they looked up, when they saw the giraffe hanging over a large branch 20 feet from the ground ; the leopard or leopards having tugged it up there.

Saunderson had, like many of us, seen large buck taken up into trees by leopards, but could not imagine how a leopard could get a carcass this size and weight up there, yet he was absolutely certain of the fact.

CHARGING LIONS

There is no rule to lay down as to when a lion will or will not charge. A very hungry or vicious lion, a lion that has been previously hunted, or shot at or wounded, may charge unprovoked. I have seen a lion charge at first sight, but, generally speaking, a lion does not charge unless he has been persistently followed on foot, ridden after, shot at or wounded. Again, generally speaking, he will not attempt

to charge from a distance from his enemy of
more than 150 yards. Most of the lion
charges I have seen have been from 100
yards or under this distance. As a rule, a lion
must have been aggravated, or feel himself
cornered or desperate before he charges. A
lioness, however, will often charge at sight
to protect her cubs, if an enemy comes
near.

Apparently lions will charge from as great
a distance as 200 yards and over, but I
think charges from this distance are usually
confined to very open country. Except when
mounted and when increasing my distance from
a lion, my own experience has been that a lion
increases his pace as he charges home, and is
not likely to pull up for anything but death;
but I could give examples from the experience
of others which show that, at any rate in a
charge from a distance of 150 to 200 yards,
a lion does not always charge straight home.
Mr. W. S. Rainsford in *The Land of the Lion*
gives a very detailed account of his first lion,
and he measured the distance from which the
lion charged; carefully measured it was 170
yards : " he came 120 of them faster than I
could have believed it possible for any badly
wounded beast to come." " *At about 50 yards* "
he " *slowed down to a trot,* and as I saw his
breast I shot full into it." Mr. Rainsford killed
his lion. But do not let any one ever count on

a charging lion slowing down to a trot in the last 50 yards.

As far as regards the question of springing, I should say that when they attack from some distance off, they often cover some of the ground in bounds, especially in grass, and when they charge they do not in their last stride actually leave the ground (though possibly this is done on occasion) with all four feet, but rear up and strike left and right with their fore-paws and seize neck or shoulders with their teeth. Most of the people, more particularly natives, whom I have seen after being mauled, or who have been spectators of lions attacking men who were standing erect, describe a lion's action in this way, in fact very much as you may see a kitten use her fore-paws when catching at a ball. Probably most sportsmen who are caught in a charge are bowled over by the rush, and know very little more than that they are on the ground with a lion growling and crunching up their arm or their leg.[1]

A friend of mine, Mr. Mervyn Ridley, who was very badly mauled two or three years ago by a lioness, described what he saw to me in this way: he had with some natives and a companion been looking for a lioness which the natives had seen go into a certain bush; after a

[1] Vaughan Kirby mentions measuring an exceptional lion's bound of 21½ feet. But I consider double this distance is at times covered in the bound of a lion. Over 40 feet has been measured.

A Charging Lion.

To face p. 176.

careful investigation of the particular bush which
the natives declared she had entered, they came
to the conclusion, after much peering and peeping,
that the natives had made a mistake, and that
she was in the next bush, and off they set to
examine one close at hand. Ridley had just
turned on his heel and was about to move off,
when the lioness flew out at him from the bush
he had just turned his back on; he had just
time to fire as she sprang in the air—though he
hit her she landed on the top of him, and the next
moment he was on the ground with the lioness
lying beside him chawing and munching his arm
from the wrist up to the shoulder, growling
while she crunched the bone.

Others being there, his life was saved, though
his sufferings from the after effects were terrible,
and lasted many weeks, and his arm crippled
for life; he had not even the satisfaction of
getting the brute's skin, for she escaped.

In 1895, when I first went to Somaliland,
I purchased the ponies and some of the camp
kit of an officer, a gunner, named Sandbach, who
had just succumbed to blood-poisoning after
being mauled by his first lion. What took place
when this accident occurred also illustrates the
behaviour of lions when attacking.

Sandbach and his shikari were standing at
the end of a grass patch where a lioness was
known to be in hiding, whilst his boys had gone
to the far end to drive her out. As they failed

to dislodge her with cries and stones, the grass
was set on fire and out she came. Sandbach's
shikari had the main supply of ammunition and
a second rifle, he himself had half a dozen cartridges or so, but expended them in shooting at
her some distance off, only hitting her once in
the belly, whereupon she charged straight at
Sandbach and his gun-bearer; the former had
only his empty rifle, and no time to reach his
second; the lioness rose at the shikari and hit
him one awful clout on the head, smashing his
skull to pieces like an egg-shell, killing him
instantaneously: then she turned at once on
Sandbach who was a tall, powerful man; he
received her attack, thrusting his rifle barrels
down her throat so far that she caught his
forward hand in her jaws—he then used his other
hand to release the one she had pinned, trying
to open her teeth, and she got hold of that arm
too; whilst thus struggling with her one of his
boys arrived, running at top speed, on the scene,
and plunged his spear into the lioness and killed
her.

In this case, had Sandbach been furnished
with the simple means of disinfecting his wounds,
or had he allowed himself to be treated by the
Somalis, whose remedies, though rough and
ready, are by no means to be despised, there
probably would have been no fatal results.
Every African hunter should have in his pocket
or saddle-bags a surgical knife, corrosive sub-

limate (or permanganate of potash, iodoform,
iodine, carbolic acid, or some other antiseptic),
a syringe, bandages, and, if possible, a silver
probe—at least a strong antiseptic should invariably be carried, and knives and bandages
steeped in it before using them. Sandbach,
not having any of these, should have submitted
to the treatment the Somalis desired to give him ;
they would at once have cut open every tooth
bite and fang stab to the bottom, and washed
them all out thoroughly with water before
binding and bandaging.

One day in 1909, while looking for some lions
near my place in British East Africa, in the
company of my daughter, and Messrs. Hume
Chaloner and Clifford and Harold Hill, the two
latter, who were driving a donga down towards
the other three of us, came upon a leopard which
one of them wounded with a ball, the leopard also
received a shot in the lungs, with a poisoned arrow,
from one of the Wakamba boys. The leopard
flew on to Harold Hill, and, fastening on his
wrist with his teeth and to his legs with his hind
claws, would no doubt have done him more
damage had not Clifford Hill (whose gun was
empty) promptly beaten the leopard off with
his gun barrels. As soon as the leopard was
disposed of, we made a solution of corrosive
sublimate, which I had in my saddle-bags, with
cold tea, as we had no water with us, and pushing
cotton wool saturated with this solution into the

punctures and wounds, we made the best job we could of it. We treated the incident as a joke, and in some respects it was an amusing accident to the parties least concerned, but we were somewhat uneasy about it, for though we did not allude to it we were all aware that the leopard, while on Hill, had had his teeth in Hill's wrist, was coughing blood over him from his lungs in which the poisoned arrow was sticking, and that this poison was of the deadliest and swiftest nature. However, the wounds healed with extraordinary rapidity without any bad effects.

This is mentioned as an instance of the ease with which very rudimentary precautions can be effectively and promptly taken. Septic poisoning is the cause of most of the fatal or serious results from the wounds made by the teeth and claws of carnivora. Men are, of course, killed outright or fatally injured by lions, never in my experience by leopards, when out shooting; but by far the greater proportion of fatalities result from blood-poisoning caused by putrefying and corrupt remnants of flesh and blood adhering to the lining of claw sheaths, or to the teeth and gums of lions and leopards.

In the case of all bites, including those of mosquitoes, flies, and ticks, especially in all tropical countries, it is a wise precaution to disinfect them at the earliest opportunity; this holds good of thorn scratches, for some thorns in Africa are very poisonous. I find on getting into camp, or on arriving home, a good wash over with a weak solution of corrosive sublimate allays irritation and heals all abrasions quickly.

The following is the account of the death of an English officer whom I knew in South Africa, and who was killed in British East Africa in his first encounter with a lion just below the hill on which my house stood. It is written by a friend of his who was present, who has asked me not to mention names, and illustrates the danger from blood - poisoning, even when claws only reach the flesh through clothing.

"On September the 27th, 1904, while travelling between Lukania and Machakos Road, Boma, we came on four lions close to the road. They at once ran to cover, only one of them show-ing; this one I shot dead at about 200 yards; two of the others cleared; these X. went after. I waited for a few minutes before going up to the one I had shot. On my way, going through some very long grass and scrub, I put up the fourth lion, and as he went away from me I shot him in the hind-quarters. He rolled over, but was on his feet again in an instant, turned round and was into the scrub in a flash, all the time making an unearthly row. I couldn't see him, and thought I had better get out of the scrub, which I did. In the meanwhile X. had no luck with the two he went after. When he returned to where I was, I told him what had happened; he then said, ' Let us get him out of it.' I said, ' No, it is too dangerous.' We waited there for a short time, thinking that the lion might shift; but no, he was lying very low. We then sent a Wakamba round, burning the grass on the top side, with the result that we could not see much for smoke. Before the fire came up to the lion, X. decided to shift his position to a place where he thought he could get a better shot. The lion was either badly shot or very sulky, for he lay in the grass until the fire burned the tuft of hair at the end of his tail. Meanwhile, from where X. was he managed to get a shot at him, hitting him low down in the belly; he got another two shots in while the brute was charging, but when the lion was close on him and he put up his rifle to fire, he evidently had got excited and forgot to reload his rifle. When the lion knocked him down, I got a bit closer and fired high at the lion, with the result that he left X. and came for me. He was very weak and did not come very quick, and as he was coming along low on the ground I had a good shot at him in the chest; he dropped quite dead. I then went up to X. and found that he had not been bitten at all, but had nineteen claw wounds on the fleshy part of his back. I tried to dress his wounds. I then fixed up a camp bed, lashed the tent poles to it and made a stretcher with it, and started a runner to Athi River station to telegraph for a doctor and a special train. We then started off with X. for the station, which was quite a job with Kikuyu porters. We arrived at the station just before the special train with the doctor. The doctor dressed X.'s wounds and we all returned to Nairobi, and X. was taken to the hospital and died there on the third day after the accident (on October 1st)."

When lions are hunting for meat they do not always kill their prey in the approved manner described in books, viz., by seizing the neck with their teeth, holding on with one fore- and the two hind-paws, and then placing the other fore-paw across the nose of the animal and pulling the head round and back, and so dislocating the neck. Having stalked or made their rush into a herd or at a single animal, they follow no fixed rule. I have seen various animals clawed on the quarters; it is common on the plains to see zebra with old or fresh marks clearly visible, every claw having left its deep line. In two instances I know of where men on horseback have been attacked, it has been from behind; on the other hand, most of the camels, horses, and antelopes which I have seen killed by lions have either had the throat or the back of the neck torn or deeply bitten.

I was in charge, as Resident Magistrate, of the Barberton District in the Eastern Transvaal between 1903 and 1905, and can vouch for the truth of the following story. I know the man well, and sat with him at times when for weeks he was recovering in bed from his strange

adventure ; every circumstance was substanti-
ated in the inquiries made, by an inspection of
the spot, and in the post-mortem examination
of the lion. It is given in Wolhuter's own
words.

CHAPTER XII

IN THE LION'S JAWS

By H. WOLHUTER, Ranger, Transvaal Government Game
Reserves.[1]

. . . ON 26th August (1904) I had to do rather
a long march on account of scarcity of water,
consequently sundown found me riding along
the native bank some three miles short of my
destination, Metzi Metz, accompanied by a large,
rough-haired dog (of no very special breed, but
of tried courage), and carrying my ·400 express.
My four natives and three donkeys were a few
miles behind me.

It was already pretty dark, twilight being a
matter of minutes in these latitudes, and the
path which I followed led along the banks of a
small dried river bed. I had reached a place
where a patch of long grass grew beside the
path, when my dog " Bull " ran forward barking,
and I caught sight of some indistinct forms
which, from their general appearance, I took to
be reedbucks ; the very last thing I was thinking

[1] Extracted from the *Journal*, vol. i., of the Society for the
Protection of the Fauna of the Empire.

of was lions, having been fruitlessly tramping
the country in hopes of securing one for some
time. I therefore whistled to the dog, and the
next moment was conscious of a lion close to me
on the off side, and preparing to spring. I had
no time to lift my rifle, but simply snatched my
horse round to the near side, and drove the
spurs in ; he gave a bound which, no doubt,
caused the lion partially to miss his spring, as
his claws slipped on the horse's quarters, and
though several ugly wounds were inflicted he
lost hold. The concussion and the subsequent
violent spring of the horse caused me to lose my
seat, and simultaneously I saw a second lion
rushing up from the opposite direction. I absolutely fell into his jaws, and believe that he had me
before I ever touched the ground. I imagine that
these lions were after the horse in the first instance,
there being no known man-eaters in the district,
but finding me so easy a prey, this gentleman
decided to accept what Providence offered to him.

The next thing I recollect was being dragged
along the path on my back, my right arm and
shoulder in the lion's mouth, my body and legs
underneath his belly, while his fore-paws kept
trampling on me as he trotted along, lacerating
the fronts of my thighs considerably and tearing
my trousers to shreds.

I had, of course, dropped my rifle, which I
was accustomed to carry in a bucket in mounted
infantry fashion. All the time the lion was

dragging me along he kept up a sort of growling purr, something like a hungry cat does when she catches a bird or a mouse, and is anticipating a welcome meal.

My spurs kept dragging and catching in the ground till at last the leather broke. I cannot say that my feelings at this time were at all in accord with those of Dr. Livingstone, who in his book, if I am not mistaken, expresses his feelings as those of dreamy repose, with no sense of pain; I, on the other hand, suffered extremely in that respect, while I hope I may never have again to undergo such agony of mind as I then experienced; it seemed hard to die like that, and yet I could see no part of a chance, not the slightest loophole of escape.

Suddenly, like a flash, I thought of my sheath knife; I always carried it in my belt behind my right hip, and on most other occasions when I had had a fall it had fallen out; was it still there? The lion holding me by the right shoulder, I was obliged to reach round and underneath me in order to get at it. It took a long time, as it must be remembered that I was being dragged and trotted on by my captor all the time, but at last I managed it. How I held on to that knife! It was only an ordinary 3-inch blade of soft steel, such as one buys cheap at any up-country store, but it meant all the world to me then. I now no longer thought of death or anything else; all my mind and energy were

concentrated on not letting go my one last road
of escape. After dragging me nearly 200 yards,
the lion stopped under a big forked tree with
large roots; as he did so, I felt for where I
judged his heart to be, and struck him behind
the shoulder—one, two—with the energy of
despair, using, of course, my left hand. He
dropped me at the first stab, but still stood
above me growling, and I then struck him a
third time in the throat with all the force of
which I was capable, severing some large vein
or artery, as the blood deluged me. On receiving
this last stab my adversary sprang away and
stood facing me two or three yards off, still growling; I scrambled to my feet, and so we stood
opposite to one another. I fully expected him
to attack me again, and, recalling what I had
often read about the effects of the human voice,
I shouted at the pitch of my lungs all the most
opprobrious epithets of which I was master. I
fear much of what I said would be quite un-
printable and quite unfit " to point a moral or
adorn a tale," but I don't think under the
circumstances that even the most pronounced
advocate of the *suaviter in modo* could have
expected me to be polite.

Perhaps the force and volume of my language
helped what my good little knife had begun, but
anyhow, after what seemed an age, and may
have been only a few seconds, the lion turned
and was lost to sight in the darkness. I could

hear his growls turning to moans, which got
fainter and finally ceased, and to my inexpres-
sible relief I felt that I had probably killed him.
Before this, however, I had lost no time in
getting up the friendly tree as expeditiously as
my lacerated right shoulder would permit me,
and was hardly safely ensconced out of danger
when the other lion, who had made a long and
unsuccessful chase after my horse, with " Bull "
sticking close and barking all the time, returned
to the spot where it had parted from its companion, immediately picked up my blood spoor,
and came with a rush nearly to the foot of my
tree. I now shouted to the dog to encourage
him, and he went for the lion in great style,
barking all round him, until the latter retreated
and disappeared for a few minutes, at the end
of which he returned and made an ugly charge
at the dog, who cleverly avoided him, and
nothing daunted, returned to the attack, en-
couraged by my shouts. Finding he could
neither get rid of his diminutive antagonist nor
yet get at me, Leo evidently thought he was
giving himself a good deal of trouble for nothing,
and so went off sulkily in the direction taken by
his now dead companion.

I was by this time feeling very faint and stiff,
and fearing I would swoon and fall from the tree,
I fastened myself to the branches as well as I
could with neckcloth and handkerchief. Presently I heard voices which heralded the arrival

of my boys. I promptly called to them, and
with their assistance got down from the tree;
it took an immense time. I was suffering from
a raging thirst and in great pain, and we had 4
miles nearly to go to camp. Roughly bandaging
my shoulder, we started off, carrying firebrands
in case the lion should return. Never shall I
forget that walk ; often I fancied I heard stealthy
footfalls in the darkness, and it seemed in my
weakness and pain as if we should never arrive.
I put the distance down at 14 miles, thinking
I was estimating it very moderately, and even
now it seems difficult to realize that it was
barely four.

However, all things have an end, and we got
to the huts at last about midnight, I suppose.
The boys ran off to get water, but, owing to the
usual pools being dry, it took a long time finding
any, and I lay enduring untold agonies of thirst.
When at last the grateful liquid did come, I
simply could not stop drinking, and don't know
why I did not do myself some serious injury.
High fever set in before morning. The boys
went out at sunrise and found my horse grazing
quietly in the bush, and not much the worse,
my rifle (a new one) uninjured, and the lion,
which proved to be an old male, with a grey-
flecked mane, his long canines worn quite flat
at the points. His stomach was quite empty,
and he must have been ravenously hungry. The
other, I should say, must have been a much

younger animal, from what I saw of him; I suppose they had had a run of bad luck hunting.

After the boys had made a litter and I had rested a day, I was carried down to Komati Poort, and promptly forwarded to Barberton Hospital, which I reached six days after the accident, and here excellent attention and comfort awaited me.

CHAPTER XIII

THE FOOD AND DRINK OF LIONS

IT is impossible to say what is the favourite
food of lions. In East Africa zebra, which is
always fat, appears to be their standing dish,
but they kill large numbers of hartebeest,
wildebeest, impala, and in fact all the antelopes from gazelle to the largest, even including sometimes the giraffe. In countries where
buffalo abound they feed largely upon them. It
is often stated in books that they eat putrid
carcasses and carrion; they will certainly eat and
are fond of elephant and rhinoceros meat, whether
fresh or " high "—these of course are beasts they
cannot kill themselves. I have known them
come to eat the corpses of giraffe and zebra, but
I feel very confident that, excepting say elephant,
rhinoceros, and giraffe, they prefer the fresh meat
of zebra, antelopes, buffalo, camel, horse, and ox
which they have killed themselves. For a man
to kill hartebeest or other antelopes and to use
the dead bodies as lion baits, or to leave out the
carcasses of oxen and horses which have not been
killed by lions, in the hope of the meal thus
provided attracting the King of Beasts, will

result in disappointment nine times out of ten ;
but to revisit the remains of rhinoceros, elephant,
and giraffe will often meet with a reward. If a
lion comes upon a beast freshly killed by sportsmen, he is very likely to make a meal off it, or
to visit it; and where lions are known to be
about in the neighbourhood, it is worth while
to sit in hiding over your kill for a few hours
within easy shot and with the wind in your face
—a hungry lion will sometimes come in broad
daylight to the carcass. A hungry lion is a bad,
bold beast ; Lord Delamere told me that once
when he was riding down a wounded oryx bull
in Somaliland and was pressing him hard, a
lion sprang out of the grass and pulled down the
oryx under his very nose.

It must again be repeated that lions' habits
vary in different localities, and when authorities
state that a lion " always " returns to his kill,
that he then drags it away before making a
second meal, and so on, these may be generalizations pretty accurate for one region and not in
another. For instance, in that part of British
East Africa with which I am most familiar,
I should say lions very seldom return to their
kill, owing to the abundance of game they kill
nightly. After disembowelling their victim,
feasting on intestinal dainties, and eating their
fill off the fattest and softest portions, they retire
towards daylight to lie up in some shelter hard
by, whilst hyænas, jackals, and vultures finish

what they leave, and the lions repeat the performance the following night.   No lion on the Kapiti Plains would find anything left of his kill to eat if he did return.

In Somaliland lions very often return to their kills, but I have often known them not to do so, and although I have frequently sat over their kills at night, I only once obtained a shot and killed a lion by this means.   On that occasion the lion had killed two big camels, and I disturbed him just at the beginning of his feast in the early morning.   I remained by the kill all that day and through the next night; he returned about the middle of the night, and I shot him.

Several lions I have killed have had porcupine quills sticking in their paws and lips; both lions and leopards seem to be fond of porcupine flesh, in spite of this kind of pepper.   Lions invading enclosures often kill a great deal more than what they require for food; instances are known of their killing a score or two of goats or sheep, and I have known about fifty ostriches killed by lions in a single night.

Mr. Selous relates an instance which came under his observation, where a lion killed one hundred pigs in a compound in a single night! But then, if I remember right, the lion had got into an enclosure he could not see the way out of, and presumably got into a state of nervous irritation which drove him to vent his annoyance

on the black squealing things that tore madly
about as he rushed round and round the boma
to find an exit. It is possible that he did it just
for sport, biting pig after pig in the neck, as I
have known a fox bite off the heads of more than
a hundred pheasants in a pheasant field in one
night. Dog should not eat dog, yet lion is said
to eat lion. I have returned to many dead lions
and seen no sign of their ever doing so, but I
do not question the experience of others on this
point. The leopard loves a dish of dead dog
of his own killing; thus cat eats dog, whether
cat eats cat or not.

Again, it is not accurate to say that lions
" always " drink water after their meals; it is
probably true they would always like to. Some
authorities state that lions always suck the
blood of the animals they kill before proceeding
to eat; I do not know anything about this, and
never heard any one say they had seen them
doing it, but apart from the question of " suck-
ing," they no doubt lap up a large quantity of
blood. Now it is inconceivable that lions, for
instance on the waterless Haud of Somaliland,
drink water even once a week in some localities,
for lions are there not only during the rains
but long after every water pool is dried up.
Naturalists will say that antelopes as well as
lions must have water to drink. I have shot a
lion far out of reach of water during an eight
days' march across the Haud, when there was

not a drop of water on the Haud.   The naturalist will say the lions know of water you do not know of ; every one who knows the Haud in the dry season will corroborate me when I assert that there cannot be possibly any water in certain regions where the lions are.   But then these sceptics would not credit the fact that the Somalis, with their camels, ponies, and flocks, will live in the Haud for months at a time, a hundred miles or so from water pools or wells, and without seeing water ; yet it is nevertheless a fact that, while there is any verdure on the prairies, with their vast herds of gale (female camels) yielding an enormous milk supply, they require for themselves no other food or drink than this nourishing, strengthening, thirst-quenching beverage, and that their ponies are never in better condition than during these months when the grass is green and they drink no water but slake their thirst out of the over-flowing milk hans.   Needless to say, Somali ponies are more immune from thirst than even most African breeds of horses ; they are accustomed to search for the moisture necessary for them, not only among the greener grass, but among the more evergreen of the Somali bushes and trees.   Nature has provided in the driest places of the earth protected and hidden reservoirs of liquid in its plant life.

Sir Edmund Loder, my wife, and I put in

nine days on one occasion in crossing the waterless Haud, where it was more than 200
miles between the southern and northern wells
(from Hagal in the south to Sheikh Aubahadleh
in the north). We had five Somali ponies, and
we rode them all day; we passed but one patch
of green grass during the nine days, where some
thunder-shower, born out of due time, had fallen
a week or two previously; our ponies had
water but twice during this anxious crossing.
Measured by hours the time taken was just about
195 hours, *i.e.* a few more hours than eight
days of twenty-four hours each. The ponies
were watered thus (the camels had no water at
all) :—

> Water " ad lib." at the starting
> from the Wells of Hagal.[1]

After 78 hours. 1½ bucket of water each.

,,   38   ,,   1 bucket each.

,,   79   ,,   Arrived at the wells at Sheikh
Aubahadleh.

————

195 hours.

Under ordinary conditions this journey should
have been made in seven days. As for antelopes
and gazelles, I have argued the water question
with the book naturalists, who know all about
these things, and in spite of them all I assert

————

[1] I have known a French officer's horse, a Saharian barb, do a
ten days' desert march on one litre of water a day and survive.

that for the antelopes and all living things, save
man, in certain vast regions of the Sahara,
where I have been, there is no water whatever
save in deep wells, and not even to oblige the
learned will these stupid animals carry long
ropes and pails about with them. But desert
herbage and plant life is curiously and wonderfully made; it is armed ingeniously in many ways,
in its surfaces, in the forms of its leaves, in the
hardness and texture of its barks, in globular
shapes and bulbous growths, beautifully devised
for their purpose; within these defences the life-
giving liquid lies safely hid, defying scorching
sun and drying wind and dust. Sheep in
England, owing to the greenness of our grass
and the moisture of our herbage, seldom drink,
practically never; in Africa their food is often
so dry and withered that the watering of the
flocks is the chief toil of the shepherds. The
natives of the Sudan bring their sheep miles
to the great rivers to water them, whilst the
Somalis and other natives of Africa bring their
cattle and sheep to the wells and draw water
for them.

That a lion can go many days without water
in a country where he is able to feed freely on
fresh flesh is a fact, and though for any lion it
may be a painful adaptation to circumstances,
he survives on such moisture as blood and the
intestines of animals provide him with. My
own opinion is that he can go several weeks

without water,[1] for it is difficult to imagine a
lion making many journeys to and from water
even 50 miles away.

[1] *Vide* pp. 138, 139, A. L. Butler's remarks on lions in waterless
districts of the Sudan. The Somalis, who are well acquainted with
the habits of lions in their country, never told me of lions on the
Haud eating the water-melons or other water-holding plants, nor
do I remember seeing any of these plants on the Haud.

CHAPTER XIV

LION-HUNTING

GORDON CUMMING says that lion-hunting is dangerous under any circumstances, but the danger can be reduced to a minimum by proper precautions. Selous declares the lion to be far more dangerous than any other animal in Africa. I have heard other experienced hunters say that you have only to go on long enough at the game to be caught. With but a slight experience of elephants and rhinoceroses and almost none with buffalo, I cannot pretend to set myself up as an authority beside the men I have named, and many others whom I know, who have had a full experience of all dangerous African game, but I suppose I have been in at the death of nearly as many lions as either of those two noted hunters ; and as far as I can judge I corroborate their opinion. However, I hope to show that it is possible, by the exercise of vigilance and the display of a respectable amount of skill, to reduce the risks of accidents very decidedly. The chief danger in lion-hunting is over - confidence and obliviousness to the risk attending the lightning rapidity of the lion's action at unexpected moments.

Lion-hunting may be conducted in a great variety of ways. I propose to consider them in the order of merit, as regards sport from my point of view :—

1. Tracking on foot ;
2. Hunting on horseback ;
3. Hunting with dogs (on foot or on horse-back) ;
4. Night shooting from zaribas and machâns by water places or over kills.

The books containing hints on hunters' equipment and armament are legion, and remarks here on this subject shall be as short as I can make them ; each man has some different idea as to what he requires for his comfort and efficiency. What clothes you wear, what arms and accessories you take with you when lion-hunting, depend on where you are, and whether you are going to hunt on foot or on horseback, by day or by night, and whether alone or attended by few or many men. On the question of weapons alone you may find a great variety of opinions among experienced sportsmen, and as a rule each man can give good reasons for his predilections. I propose to outline mine.

To begin with, I would, if possible, always have a good pony ; by " good " I mean a pony that answered as nearly as I could get one to this description, namely, as handy as a first-rate polo pony, absolutely steady under all conditions of fire, standing stock-still at the shortest notice, never wincing at shots fired near him, from his back when at rest, or between his ears and past his eyes when he has been given the bridle and you shoot at full gallop, a pony that is fast and free, that will turn and bend, is sure of foot and will jump off from rest like a racehorse, whenever the signal to go is given. Of course in many places among mountains and rocks, in thick bush and forest countries, these qualities cannot be of much service, and your pony becomes a mere fatigue-saving accessory, enabling you to carry more, to go farther and get back to camp after the hardest day. In case of accident to yourself or boys, the presence of a pony or its absence may make the difference between life and death. If you are hunting in the open, you had better hunt on foot than on an impetuous hard-mouthed, stumbling or shying brute, or even on a slow and spiritless animal. In either of these cases you run the extra risk of being caught ; your horse may become unmanageable at a critical moment, or go heels over head, or refuse to allow you to shoot, swerving when you are on his back, trying to break away from you when you are dismounted, perhaps not allowing you to mount, or being so stupid that he will neither attempt to carry you nor himself out of danger. I have seen a good man on a good pony very nearly caught just because the pony had not size, strength, or pace to carry such a load out of danger. I recommend a colonial pattern,

panelled saddle with wallets or small saddle-bags.
In your saddle-bags you can carry spare ammunition, knives, lunch, antiseptics, anything you
want with you, but do not stuff big saddle-bags
full and overweight your pony, and see they
are adjusted so as not to swing when you gallop.
Look to it that your stirrup leathers are sound
and your stirrup irons large and heavy, heavy
irons which leave your boots free in them, drop
off your foot in a fall and minimize the risk of
being dragged. I always carry a leather-punch
and a few bifurcated rivets for mending bridles,
girths, etc. Where there is riding and galloping
to be done, the dress I find most convenient is
this: very hard rubber-soled boots, the shortest
necked spurs I can get (long spurs are liable to
trip you up when walking), canvas leggings,
khaki drill riding or knickerbocker breeches,
Norfolk jacket with leather belt (the latter run
through one of the shoulder straps of your field-
glass case, to prevent it swinging when riding or
tumbling forward when crawling), the pockets of
the coat strong-lined for cartridges and to button
down (three pockets inside, three pockets outside), and a khaki Elwood skikar helmet with a
chin strap that fits. I carry besides skinning
knives in my saddle-bags, one strong camp
knife with tin opener, corkscrew, buttonhook, and
screw-driver; I have long since discarded re-
volvers as intolerable, nearly useless and dangerous lumber, my little Mannlicher is always on

my back or in my hand. One acquaintance of
mine carries a double-barrelled 12-bore pistol
as his last resort with lions, a capital weapon,
no doubt, but a tiresome addition to one's load
in a hot country; but he was once bitten badly
by a lion, and "once bit by lion more than twice
shy" holds good for most people.

Many of the best men hunt in their shirts
without coat or waistcoat, in breeches cut short
like bathing drawers, and with bare legs. To
me this fashionable costume is the height of
discomfort and very unpractical, necessitating
hanging your middle round with bandoliers,
pouches and knife cases, and stuffing your
breeches pockets with all sorts of things; also
a constant hitching up of your breeches and
stuffing down of your shirt. When the shirt
sleeves are cut off at the shoulder and your legs,
in a hot climate, are wound round and round in
thick woollen putties, the misery is complete,
but it must be borne if you would have your
arms, as well as your knees, tanned brown, not
forgetting neck and chest. Remember, the
browner your arms and chest, and the more
ticks and bites you can show on your knees,
the finer fellow you are; but personally I should
be happier in nothing but a coat and pair of
trousers. As to rifles, I prefer to have one
light handy rifle and a double-barrelled ball
and shot gun carried in reserve, when after lions.
The rifle which has been my constant companion

since 1892 is a rather short barrelled, five shot
magazine ·256 Mannlicher; any apparent de-
ficiency in size of bore and weight of bullet is
compensated for, in my opinion, by the ease and
rapidity with which it can be manipulated, the
little room occupied by ammunition, the flatness
of the trajectory and the superiority of its
striking energy over some of the larger bores.
With the ·256 I have killed many lions as well
as pachyderms, and antelopes from greater
kudu downwards, it is no weight to carry on
foot or on horseback, and the mechanism is of
the simplest and strongest kind; wet, sand, mud,
tumbles, and croppers have never injured it, and
a soft-nosed bullet or a ratchet H.P.[1] Fraser's
ball " sets up " so well that at times it makes
a hole almost as big as one of nearly double its
calibre. My gun-bearer carries as a rule a very
out-of-date weapon, namely, a double-barrelled
10-bore ball and shot hammer-gun, shooting
black powder and solid soft, solid hard, and
H.P.[1] bullet; it is accurate up to 100 yards, it
has always served its purpose well with me on
lion, elephant, and rhino, and though un-
wieldy has done execution with small shot as
well as with buckshot. I once shot thirteen
guinea-fowl with the two barrels! Of course, to
use such a weapon is almost laughable nowadays,
but I feel so very safe behind it, and have seen it
give lions such smashing blows when it blazes,

[1] H.P. = Hollow Point.

bangs and booms forth, that I have no inclination
to discard it, for what I admit are the more
beautiful, more powerful, and more accurate
cordite rifles of the day. But remember there
are at least two things to be said; whilst the
accuracy, flat trajectory and great range of a
powerful modern rifle give it an immense general
superiority over old-fashioned guns and express
rifles, much of this superiority is lost when in
action at a rapidly moving object at, say, 25
yards or less range. With a charging lion,
there is no time for carefully aligning delicate
sights; to hit and to hit true once and twice is
more easy with a heavy old big-bore rifle or gun
than with a powerful, short-barrelled sharp re-
coiling ·450 or ·500 cordite rifle. At such close
range the former does all that is necessary, and, in
my opinion, does it better, because there is the
risk of the modern more powerful rifle driving
its cased bullet through and beyond the animal,
in fact drilling it, whereas with a soft, solid lead
ball, the ball " sets up " at once, flattening and
mushrooming without splintering and breaking
up (in the way a soft-nosed, cordite rifle bullet
or hollow point one so often does), and the soft
lead ball goes ploughing and smashing on till the
whole force of the blow is expended *in* the
animal, *i.e.* the lion gets it *all*. The penetration
and energy of a cased bullet in front of modern
explosives is not necessarily an advantage at
close quarters with lions; there is not always

sufficient resistance to a high velocity metal enveloped projectile to " set it up," and there is a risk of its piercing through and wasting a large proportion of its force beyond the important part of the target or right beyond the target altogether. I certainly am of opinion that the safest weapon to use at close quarters is a handy double-barrelled weapon with soft lead ball in both barrels or ball in the right and shot in the left. As to what sized shot, I incline to think that any size above No. 4 up to S.S.S.G. will do ; if you can wait till a lion is, say, within 3 yards before you pull the trigger of your last barrel, I believe No. 1 would be as effective as any size, and that even No. 4 or No. 5 would be good enough.

I have noticed one or two of the most experienced of my acquaintance discard everything but an ordinary 12-bore shot gun, loaded with treble A (AAA) or a similar size of shot, for close quarters ; and facing a ferocious lion I have felt quite comfortable with my ·256 Mannlicher in my hand and a 12-bore gun, loaded with big shot, cocked on the ground between my feet.

The great thing is to be able to hit a lion accurately where it is certain to stop him, and it is better to use a small-bore rifle that you know and can shoot well and quickly with, than a bigger one which you do not feel perfectly at home with. Let every man use the weapons he knows best and believes in ; the choice is

great, and the rifles of the day are wonderful.
I cannot see why an effective shot and ball
weapon for modern powders cannot be produced,
say 20-bore or 16-bore, weighing not more than
8¼ lb., which would be handy to ride and shoot
with, combining the accuracy of a rifle up to
300 yards, with the stopping power of a gun
at close range; something of the sort has
been produced by Westley Richards. I have
seen his 28-bore and heard nothing but praise of
it, but it is a small bore for shooting small game
like partridges and francolin, and I hanker after
a big soft lead ball.

Rifle makers do not quite understand the
kind of weapon you want for shooting from a
galloping horse one minute and the next minute
on foot at over 200 yards range at a galloping animal, and a few minutes later at an
animal charging from thirty yards distance.
One eminent gunmaker suggested to me that I
should find a telescopic sight very useful for
this work! Fancy bounding over cracks and
mounds at full speed trying to sight a flying
animal through a telescope, or even a great
lumbering, galloping beast only forty yards off,
when it is all you can do, standing in your
stirrups with a clean level short barrel to get
the line and catch your game on the hop; for
as your horse rises and falls in his stride your
muzzle saws up and down. Even with your
target dead straight in front of you, or exactly

parallel on your left, it is not always easy to snap off at the right moment. What you really do, I think, is instinctively to pull just before the moment that you see your rifle muzzle is going to fall down to the object or going to rise on to it; personally I try to get within 15 yards of anything but lion, before I fire at full gallop, and at this range, or under, it is easy work even to kill small beasts such as jackal, but when much over this range it is "chancy," though even then the shot comes off more often than you would expect.

Solid rubber-soled boots are the best for hunting in, they are the most comfortable to walk in, the most noiseless, give a splendid foothold when climbing rocks and boulders in dry countries; Indian sambur leather cotton-soled boots are excellent for hot, dry, and fairly level countries like Somaliland, but give poor foothold on grassy slopes in East Africa and get nasty in countries where there is rain or the hunter has to wade through dew-covered grass. If you must have brown knees to display, no doubt you can get used to shooting in bathing drawers and may come to enjoy crawling over thorn-beds in bare legs and the titillation of insects. If you desire full protection to your legs and do not mind how hot they are, leather leggings are excellent. I prefer canvas, as giving much more freedom and coolness—for putties I have no use whatever, life is too short for their adjustment.

In hot countries I regard them as unbearable ;
unless time and pains are taken in putting them
on, they will be a source of continual worry all
day.   I have seen a man hurrying after a wounded
buck holding the end of undone yards of his
putty in his hand and getting the thing caught
in thorns and branches—an object for sympathy.

A sufficient party to take out for a day's
hunting with you in Africa would be one composed
of a syce for your pony, a reliable gun-bearer or
shikari, and a third boy or second gun-bearer.   A
syce should never get out of touch with you and,
besides looking after your pony when you are
mounted, should carry your water-bottle or
anything else you may want, such as a camera
or telescope.   A No. 8 prism binocular you should
carry yourself.   If you want to send in a quantity
of meat to camp, of course you require more
boys, or camels, or mules, according to the
country you are in.

I have seen the best of sportsmen mar their
chances by having a number of boys with them,
carrying stools, cameras, luncheons, a variety of
arms and other things.   As some men think they
cannot shoot standing in long grass a camp-stool
is a great comfort to them, but after all, in Africa
you *must* shoot standing up very frequently
indeed, and even if you can get seated on a stool
and have it brought up to you without disturbing
the animals you are stalking, you are without
the same command and extent of vision that you

have when erect, and are, of course, far less free
to follow moving objects and to adapt your
shooting to their movements. Erect, you see
your sights more clearly, as well as what you are
shooting at, and if you are not quite so steady as
sitting, there are, except for long shots, com-
pensating advantages.

No ordinary European can expect to attain the
rapidity of fire of, say, Afrikanders. This free
shooting, whether mounted or on foot and in any
position, is their chief superiority over experienced European shots. No amount of practice
on ranges, nor military training, will ever make
Europeans a match in these respects for the
settlers in the British African colonies. The
South African colonist often is reared, so to
speak, from childhood with a rifle in his hand ;
the very thing, namely, the extermination of the
big and *more easily* killed game, which people
at home have thought must have impaired the
skill of Afrikanders, has, in my judgment, done
nothing of the sort—for the buck, which remain
still in great numbers, are smaller targets and
require more skill to obtain than the big game
which once swarmed over the land. The shooting man in South Africa gets " on " with a rifle
as quickly as we do with a shot gun ; he does not
bother with back-sights and ranges as we do,
he instinctively knows what he is doing. As a
sportsman he is often not beyond reproach, as
his ability tempts him to pump lead at flying

bunches of game, and he is too often heedless of anything but of hitting *something*, careless of age and sex; the traditions of the hide and biltong hunter still cling to him. For instance, he will do with comparative ease, and with vastly better chance of success, what we attempt with hesitation and only achieve by more or less of a fluke. He will see a galloping buck 400 yards away, and before you can say "knife" his first shot strikes a yard behind the buck; you have hardly marked the puff of dust, when a second bullet strikes two yards in front or a yard over, and as quickly come two more shots in succession, one bullet correcting the preceding shot on the instant, with a nice estimate of the pace the buck is travelling. In the time five shots have been fired, one of which hits, you could not have done more than made a tolerable guess at the range, aligned your sights, judged the pace and got one or at most two shots off. Presuming you are as good a judge of range and of taking in front, he yet has some five chances to your one of scoring a hit.

In this way, by pumping lead at game moving at 500 or even 600 yards, an Afrikander will often get a buck; it is deplorable to have to assert that he will, when firing in this way at bunches of antelope, as often wound several without killing any. Yet I have seen some very bad shots among these people too!

The lion-hunter should pay attention to one

or two little details, the neglect of which has often led to fatal results. He should carry on his person sufficient ammunition for each of the weapons he has out, and so disposed that he can quickly get at each description without having to divert his eyes. I find the handiest plan is to have in my right-hand jacket pocket spare clips of ·256 cartridges and two or three 10-bore cartridges. In my left, half a dozen 10-bore and one clip of ·256—no mistake can then be made in pulling out at once with either hand what is wanted at a moment's notice. It is just as well to have a spare cartridge or two of each sort in an inside pocket, for I have several times emptied my outside pockets, in taking a head-over-heels toss, when galloping. Your gun-bearer also should have a good supply of ammunition and a further reserve may be carried in your saddle-bags. I have expended as many as, perhaps more than, twenty-five cartridges over a single wounded lioness before securing her, and then there was another lion to tackle afterwards. I have been out with others when we had to send back miles tor ammunition after killing one lion, before we had enough to follow up two or three others. The killing of a lion is often a very simple business, and authorities will declare that a lion is more easily killed than antelope ; this is not true, but it is true he is as easily killed as an antelope when it is within 30 yards range ; but a lion will carry as much lead as a kongoni, a peculiarly tough beast with extraordinary reserves of vitality, at long range shooting. Lions frequently appear to be very easily killed because you often have a very near and easy shot at them. Yet if any beast gets over the shock of the first shot, its vitality often appears to be raised to the highest pitch, and unless a subsequent shot is in heart, spine, or brain it is perfectly awful what a number of shots it may take to dispatch it.

As one out of many instances I could give of the amount of lead a lion will carry, and to discredit the common and very dangerous theory that lions are more easily killed than antelopes, I select the following. I do so as Captain Arthur A. Slatter, who writes it, is an exceptionally good shot, and Mr. Humphery besides being a good shot is, like Captain Slatter, an experienced hunter :—

" On looking through my diary for 1908 I find the page for 26th of May marked with broad red ink lines, and in the column reserved for recording game killed, an item ' 1 lion ' similarly underlined in red. The entry for the day reads as follows : ' Very exciting day, started at 6.30 a.m. with Humphery and fifty native beaters to drive dongas for lions. Saw 4, and while after these spotted a fine male lion, which we followed ; I wounded him first shot, and we then hunted him for four hours and finally bagged him. During this time he badly

mauled a beater, charged me, and in spite of
receiving a ·400 (cordite) in the mouth at four
yards, knocked me down without hurting me
much, chased Humphery and a native policeman.
Measurement 9 ft. 3 in., fine yellow mane.
Returned to camp 12 noon."

The above entry brings vividly before my
mind the incidents that took place on this red-
letter day, and I will endeavour to put them on
paper.

The District Commissioner of Machakos (Mr.
Humphery) was staying a few days at my place
at Kilima Kiu near Machakos road, and, taking
advantage of the fact that two guns are safer
than one at a lion shoot, we decided to have a
try for lions. Having assembled our Wakamba
native beaters on the previous evening, we were
enabled to make a start at dawn, a great advantage, for to my mind the first two hours of
daylight are worth all the remainder of the day
in a warm climate. There is always during these
early hours a chance of " spotting " lions on
their night's kill, in the open, or seeing them
moving towards the locality in which they intend
lying up for the day. Scent is also better for
the dogs, and, last but not least, the air is always
cool and refreshing.

Our beaters made quite a good line, which
was stiffened at intervals by a few native police-
men, whose blue uniforms and scarlet fezes
contrasted with the dirty blankets of the raw

natives. Our first drive was a likely, well-wooded and deep ravine, which lies on the northern extremity of this property ; this proved a blank. While moving away across a couple of miles of open ground to another likely beat, we saw four lions, all maneless ones, moving away from us in front in the open. Watching them go into a wooded donga, we started off in that direction. On our way we noticed the harte-beests scattering in all directions on our left, and on looking through our field-glasses made out the cause of the commotion. A fine maned lion was moving slowly up the slope of the hill on our left ; on the top of this rise it was merely covered with scrub, and we considered it probable that this old lion was going to lie up there for the day. We watched him carefully till we saw him enter the bushes, and after waiting some time and seeing no signs of him coming out, we decided to abandon the other four lions for the present and pay our attentions to this one. First of all, we sent the beaters a long wide circle, to get to the opposite side of the hill and beat up to the top and on towards us. While they were moving round, Humphery and I with our gun-bearers were, by taking advantage of a fall in the ground, enabled to get up to the edge of the bushes where we thought it most probable the lion would break cover. Here we took up our positions, each behind a thorn bush, and waited the coming of the beaters. Soon they were to be heard making a great din as they advanced towards us. A few moments later, some low deep grumbling sort of growls told us that the lion had been disturbed—almost immediately I caught sight of his majesty coming straight in our direction; getting a fairly good chance from my position, I fired with my ·400-bore. The bullet thudded well, and a succession of quick angry grunts informed me that I had hit him. At the same time he turned sharp to the left, affording Humphery a snapshot between the bushes; whether this took effect I could not say. For several minutes now we lost sight of the lion and were expecting him to make himself known in our near vicinity at any moment, but he seemed anxious to avoid us, and we soon saw him making up a slope on our left to a bush-clad piece of rising ground, similar to the one he had just vacated. The driving operation was repeated as before. This time the lion broke out at the left flank, only giving Humphery a very indifferent shot; then he stole through some thorn bushes, showing glimpses of himself now and then; at these we indulged in some snap shooting with no apparent result. After a few moments he came out and passed over some open ground, but too far off, and finally entered a small shallow dry water-course studded here and there with bushes; here he disappeared and evidently had lain down.

Now we knew the fun was to begin. Hurrying

on, we called a halt about 150 yards from where he was. Now came the question how to get the lion to show himself. We knew he was within 150 yards of us and could not get away without exposing himself, but he might have been ten miles off for all we could see of him. We could not send the beaters where we would not go ourselves, and it would have been courting disaster to have gone in to a hunted and wounded, and no doubt angry, lion. Several charges of buckshot fired into the bushes brought no response. Then remembering that nothing has such an effect on all wild animals as the human voice, I instructed the beaters—who at this stage were getting a bit nervous and had clustered round us—to shout long and loud and all together. This they did, and it acted like magic, for before they had got half-way through their shout they were instantly silenced by the deeper voice of the old lion, who suddenly made his appearance, charging straight at us all with huge bounds and uttering terrific roars with each ; the natives fled in every direction, but one ! throwing away sticks and blankets as they did so.

The lion quickly covered the 150 yards and seemed alongside us in no time; he entirely ignored Humphery and myself, no doubt keeping his eyes on the flying beaters. Humphery stood near me as I sat down, which is the position I prefer to shoot in. Humphery

fired his ·450 and I think hit all right—but no
effect whatever. In endeavouring to get a
head shot in, which I thought easy at such
range, not fifteen paces, I took a little too far in
front : the bullet smashed a large upper front
tooth out and then passed out of the cheek on
the opposite side. Though a soft nose it did not
check the lion in the least—a couple more
bounds brought him right among the terrified
beaters. Singling out one wretch, he reared
high on his hind - legs, coming down with his
paws on the native's shoulders and bringing
his man to earth and lying on the top of him
like a cat on a mouse. Things were beginning
to look serious when Humphery, no doubt
thinking to put a stop to them and prevent
further damage being done, picked up his 12-bore
shot-gun (which he had wisely kept on the ground
beside him instead of entrusting it to a gun-
bearer), which was loaded with a round bullet in
the right barrel and S.S.S.G. in the left, and
ran up to within six paces of the lion; when
practically standing over the lion, which was
still on the native, he discharged both barrels
in quick succession. We discovered afterwards
that in the excitement of the moment he missed
with the ball, but that the charge of big shot
went right into the lion's near shoulder and
withers. This was by no means the knock-out
blow, however, and appeared only to add to the
fury of the already enraged beast, which on

receiving the charge raised itself, and turned its head up sideways facing Humphery with mouth wide open, assuming an expression of savage hatred and defiance impossible to describe, at the same time uttering an earth-shaking roar. Humphery now having an empty gun and a lion snarling at him within six paces, did the only thing possible under the circumstances and bolted. The lion seemed loth to leave his victim, and still lay on the native instead of following Humphery as one would have expected.

All this had taken place in a much shorter time than it can be described; indeed, I had only just time to get another cartridge into my rifle, when to my great concern the lion left the native and charged straight at me as I sat in my original position facing him. He had about twenty paces to come, and I felt confident of being able to stop him with my big rifle. As he bore down on me head down and tail up, bleeding profusely from my previous shot, with a huge red smudge under his left eye where the bullet had come out, he was by no means a pleasing spectacle. To add to the effect, he gave forth quick, infuriated grunts as he came. I had just time to realize that he had got me all right, and to hold the rifle in a position in which it might be possible for the muzzle to enter his mouth. Then there was a huge mass of yellow hair, blood and white teeth on the top of me; the next instant I saw stars, being knocked flying on to my back by the force of the impact. My relief was not small when I found the lion had passed on without stopping to maul me in his mad fury, and was now making for Humphery and a native constable, who were about 40 yards behind me. Quickly picking myself up I grasped my rifle, which had been thrown some 5 yards from me, only to find it hopelessly choked with sand and dirt at muzzle and breech, and temporarily useless. Shouting for my gun-bearer with my ·303, I discovered not a native was in sight with the exception of a single native policeman armed with a Martini, who had remained by Humphery. To these two the lion was rapidly making, and eventually singled out the native policeman, who fled for his life, " casting away his arms in the presence of the enemy " as he did so. Now took place one of the most exciting chases ever witnessed. The native got but a poor start, but I have never seen a native run in any part of Africa as this one did, doubling and turning for about 150 yards, he described about a half circle, the lion at his heels, and to me it appeared as if he must reach the native with his forepaws at each bound; but the poor beast must have been feeling the effect of his recent bombardment and could not have been in his best running form, for after an exciting run he abandoned the chase and eventually stood eyeing Humphery and myself at about 130 yards distance, looking very nasty and full of fight. Humphery and I were now in a very unpleasant position; he had nothing but a shot gun, his gun-bearer having fled with my own, and I was totally unarmed. Every moment we expected the lion to make another charge; to have retired would have only been to encourage him to do so. We stood facing him for what seemed an interminable time, probably three or four minutes, whilst shouting to our gun-bearers to return with our rifles. They both crept up looking very sheepish and as white as natives can. Taking our rifles, we both fired at the lion, which had not moved a muscle with the exception of angry swishes of his tail; angry grunts followed, and we discovered afterwards that my ·303 had got him right on the tip of his nose. The old fellow had swallowed too much lead to come again. Shaking his head, he lopped off a couple of yards and disappeared into a thick thorn bush out of sight and, we imagined, lay down.

Both glad of a little breathing-space, we turned our attention to the injured native, whom we found badly clawed in the shoulders and back, so sent off to my horse, a distance of about one and a half miles, for water and dressings. I also carefully examined myself for scratches, but not a sign of one was to be found, though my clothes were well splashed with blood from the lion; also my left wrist was bruised, having probably come in contact with the lion's jaw and shoulder as he knocked me over. The force of the impact had bruised and scraped off the skin of my forearm under my coat, which was of fairly thick tweed.

We now sat down and had a smoke, deciding that we were no further forward than before the first charge was made. True, the lion had more lead in him, but he seemed to be either possessed or armour-coated. Against this, we had lost the confidence of our beaters, and indeed the beaters themselves.

After a short spell we renewed the attack with caution, firing into the bush into which the lion had disappeared. The first few shots brought forth low grunts, which became fainter. At last a charge of buckshot at 50 yards bringing no response, we advanced with great caution at the ready. The lion lay well in the centre of the thicket, quite dead.

It was a long time before we could persuade the natives to return and assist in dragging him out of the bush, in spite of our assurances that he was dead. When they did summon up enough courage we found a splendid specimen of a full-grown lion in perfect condition. Doubtless he was the hero of many contests, for his skin bore traces of old scars here and there. Now it was twelve noon, and the question arose whether to return to the house for lunch, or proceed after the other four lions seen previously. The natives decided the question by point-blank refusal to hunt any more, and, if the truth be told, I am not so sure that we were both so keen for more lions that day. Anyway, we knew that lunch was more important than lions. We carefully watched the skinning of the beast and recovered no less than thirteen bullets, ·450, ·400, and ·303; many of them were in the chest cavity. Indeed the shooting had been by no means bad; all the shots, with the exception of one, which had broken the off hind-leg low down, were well forward in the shoulder and head. Seven S.S.S.G. were recovered, lodged in the muscle of the near shoulder. Left side of jaw broken and both eye teeth smashed; the lungs shot through and through. Though we were undoubtedly lucky not to have received more damage from the beast, we were also unlucky in not getting a bullet into a vital spot. Curiously enough, not one had touched the brain, heart, or spine, though going very near. He was indeed a plucky lion, and fought a good fight against "fearful odds." We can only hope that he has numerous children and grandchildren who, in their turn, will afford such sport as he did. Personally, I have no wish to be quite so near to them. The native policeman assured me with pride that he discharged his Martini at the lion when he knocked me over. This being so, I was in as much danger from him as the lion, for they are notedly bad shots. The injured native has quite recovered, and is often to be seen about here, but still bears ugly scars."

One sometimes reads a statement in a paper such as this : A man says he has " killed nine lions, one after another, stone dead with a single shot each, with a ·256 rifle." You may believe it or not, but if it is credible and strictly accurate, you would not know which to envy most, his skill or his luck, but you might well expect sooner or later to hear a very different account, for such an experience is likely to prove a very dangerous one. Lions are often very difficult shots indeed ; offering a snapshot in thick bush when bolting through cover, or even when going from you in the open they expose a very narrow moving target at 250 yards or more. A lion may stand in the grass 150 yards off, with only the top of his head from his eyes up-wards visible, and that very badly defined in pale grass the same tint as his skin. In these and many other cases, even if you are not blown with running, and quite cool, the chances are even that if you hit him you wound and do not kill him, however neat a shot you may be, and then the real trouble begins. Just think what is likely to follow : the lion, wounded, say, in the back ribs or belly, swiftly turns and comes grunting and thundering down on you like a thunderbolt, so fast that were you able to draw a bead on him you would run a great risk of shooting over him, and if you fail to stop him, he is on you before you know where you are. I knew a man, a brave one, thus charged by a wounded lion he was facing, who never fired at all, but was bowled over with a loaded rifle in his hand, and mortally injured. If you have but one barrel left, your best chance is to hold it till he is within half a dozen yards or so. But suppose the wounded lion, as is more likely, does not charge at once, but slinks off growling into the grass or bush and then in silence watches you—in such places a lion may elude the most practised eye, and whilst you are wading into high grass or peering into thick places, he may seize his opportunity and you in the same instant. An experienced lion-hunter thinks a bit before he follows a wounded lion into high grass, unless he has absolutely located him to a yard, and can keep his mark; otherwise he votes it a " mug's game," and a man is not necessarily a coward because he decides that it is better to go home empty and watch for the vultures the next day, than to be a cripple for the remainder of his days.

When you are out for recreation, if this is cowardice, better to be a coward for five minutes than disabled for the rest of your life. When you can locate a lion in grass accurately and can mark the place, it requires a little practice to glue your eye to the spot where he went down out of sight, and to proceed to it without allowing anything to unglue it or to distract your attention for an instant. It requires sharp eyes to detect a lion slinking off as you draw on, and if you make a mistake he may be behind you and on your back before you can face round. As a matter of fact most beginners, and those who have had easy times with lions generally, take all these chances and usually escape scot-free. The very thing the experienced man hesitates about doing, the inexperienced will do, and often with impunity; on the other hand, the very thing the inexperienced will not do, or hesitates to do because it appears too dangerous, the experienced will do because it is the least danger-ous thing to do. For instance, if you see your way to get up very close to a lion without dis-turbing him, your chance of knocking him out in the first round is much better at 25 yards than at 100 yards or longer range.

I put tracking lions down on foot without the aid of dogs first, because it is a form of sport which requires more skill, greater effort, and is a bit more risky than hunting them with dogs and beaters or riding them down. There are many parts of Africa where tracking lions is difficult or impossible, owing to the nature of the ground. In many parts of Equatorial Africa where it might be possible for a clever tracker to follow the spoor, the natives are so useless at spooring, or so wanting in the right instinct for persevering on a line, that it is scarcely worth while to enlist their services. Some parts of the

Somali, Danakil, Galla countries, and of the Sudan
are the best regions I have seen for tracking.
The soft, light soil and open ground in very many
districts will allow the sportsman with very little
practice to track well and fast. Many of the
Somalis are excellent trackers in their own
country, and the aboriginal Midgans of that
land are bad to beat. In South Africa an
occasional native is a good spooler, and some
white men are experts too. I know nothing
about Red Indians, but believe that certain
Arabs in North Africa would prove a match
for any men in the world. In Algeria I have
had one or two Arab hunters with me who were
wonderful at tracking game on hard and rocky
ground, not an overturned pebble and scarcely
a bitten or broken blade of grass would escape
their notice. When hunting the Barbary wild
sheep, I have been astounded how one of these
men would unravel the route of larrowi or admi
on stony mountains. I recollect one day in the
Aures having at dawn found fresh traces of an
old ram, when we followed him for several miles
over ground where my fairly practised eye only
now and again saw evidence that we were going
right. After a long interval, during which I saw
not the faintest indication that we were on
his track, my Arab took off his sandals and
whispered, " He is very near, just in front of
us." " Have you seen him ? " I asked. " No,
but he is close to us." A minute or two later

we crossed a ridge, and there he was below us. Subsequently I asked him how he knew he was near. He took me back a few hundred yards and took hold of a tiny twig of green bush and said, "Look at that"; the end was nibbled off, the sap still wet, and an inch or so of the green stem still shining with damp. He had marked this with his eye without ever halting or turning.

It is not mere eye with these men, but a development of the same instinct that you may observe in a good huntsman who has a generally correct idea of the line of a fox. Equally wonderful are the nomads of the Sahara. In the Erg and sandy regions of the great desert, tracking may appear to be a simpler art. For those who have eyes to see, the doings of every beast and reptile are plainly written on the face of the earth. In the Souf Desert, when I was with Sir Edmund Loder in search of the rime, the gazelle which now bears his name (*Gazella loderi*), we had a negro hunter who tended the flocks of his owner, called "Ibrahim," as merry, agile, and wiry a bit of stuff in the slave line as ever lived on camel's milk and dates. We tempted him to guide us to the country of the rime; he did this, and proved himself a marvel in many ways. He was among other things the best time-reader of spoor I ever saw; he would select one in twenty tracks by a touch of the spoor with his big toe, and inform you at once whether it was half an hour or four hours old. I got him to try and explain how touching with his toe a gazelle track told him so much. He said it was difficult to enlighten me, but selecting several tracks he showed me this much : During the night, whether there was much or little dew, the dew remained on the ground for a longer or shorter time. If there was dew on the footprint as well as on the ground around the track, the gazelle had passed before dawn and while dew was still falling. If dew had fallen on the footprint, then as soon as the sun was up it slightly caked, with a thin skin of adhering sand, the surface of the heel or frog of the footprint : he could feel this slight crust with a light touch of the toe or finger. When the toe had touched it the crust was broken, and the broken edges of the crust were visible to the eye. If, however, there was no crust on the footprint and the sand ran at once to the touch of his toe, the gazelle had passed after the sun was up. As to how far the gazelle might be ahead, he judged from the sharpness of the track, for soon after a footprint is made in dry sand, the grains begin to run down the steeper indentations of the track and gradually fill up such deep little grooves as are left by the points and edges of the hoof.

One night when my wife and I were travelling in the Sahara, and were camped at Ain Melala, between the country of the Beni M'zab and Ouargla, I started a topic as we sat over the camp fire which led to an amusing

competition among our men (Arabs, Somalis,
and Chambas), each man claiming for his own
countrymen a superlative skill in tracking. We
had begun by inquiring of Ben Messaoud, our
Chamba Mehari cavalier, how the Chamba could
find their way in the sand dunes of the Areg.
His reply was : When there were no tracks of the
route there was generally here and there particles
of camel-dung floating on the top of the sand,
if caravans had passed that way within recent
years, but that some of them could find their
way by feeling the sand, or by noticing its
colour, as in different localities it differed in
texture and tint. He summed it up by saying :
" Every man knows his own country, and this is
our country." I remarked that the Soufis were
very good trackers. Mohamed Ali (my Somali
servant) said the Somalis could tell if a lion had
passed in the morning, afternoon, or previous
night ; and I said our negro " Ibrahim " could tell
the date and hour of a gazelle track by touching
it with his toe. The Chamba said that they could
tell at once if any member of their tribe lost a
camel, who the camel belonged to, and which
camel it was, by its track, even if its track was
mixed up with hundreds of others and went for
days. Ben Backai (my Arab shikari) said Arabs
could tell if a gazelle was with young or not by
its track. The Chamba then said he knew two
men of his tribe who came upon a hare track.
One said, " Look ! this is the track of a hare that

is with young." The track went into some bush and thick grass ; they went round it, and took up the track again beyond it, whereupon the other remarked, "This is not the track of the same hare we tracked on the other side, for this one is *not* with young." "Yes," said the first, "it is the same, and if we go back we shall find the young one in the bush;" and going, it was even as he said, and there was a newly born leveret in the grass. What amused me was my boy Mohamed Ali's translation, for I asked him to render into English certain points in this story which were beyond my grasp. He called the little leveret a "kid" throughout, and translated being with young: "a hare wid a kid in his billy."

TRACKING LIONS

Somaliland has a character and wildness all its own : you travel with camels, the best of all transport animals, and once away in the interior the sportsman is monarch of all he surveys, and could wander there for years without being interrupted by any reminder that there was a world outside. At least it was so in my day. Let the reader suppose himself there, that it is dawn in camp, breakfast eaten (never hunt in the tropics on an empty inside), and your two shikaris, your syce and pony standing at his tent door to receive his rifles, water-bottle, and ammunition. You mount your little Somali

pony and ride out of camp rifle in hand, with
your shikari in front carrying your heavier
weapon; the camels are also going out with
their escort, to feed in the bush all day. It is
pleasant at sunrise in the limitless Somali bush,
with the light catching a myriad bulbous thorns,
shining like silver on the galol trees, with here
and there in the glades the dark, glistening green
of the weeping kedi bushes. In this light the
red of the dar flowers is like fire, and the points
of the bayonet-leaved aloes like burnished steel.
This is the hour when the birds are all astir,
and the warblers busy in the flat tops of the
great red-stemmed mimosa trees; doves and
sand-grouse sweep past overhead to or from their
morning drink and bathe at the pool hard by
the camp. The soil here is sandy and red, the
trees mostly stunted and grey branched, giving
the impression of being in a sort of interminable
orchard, but as you wind in and out amongst
them, you pass, now and again, a great high
thicket of ergin and places dense with garlands
and streamers of armo and other creeping and
trailing things. Suddenly the head shikari looks
at the ground, turns left handed, and then halts
and says in a low tone, " Libah " (lion). In a
moment you are off your pony examining the
track. Yes, it is quite fresh; there are two lions,
one a large one by the spoor. A word to the
syce to keep well behind, a look at the rifles to
see that they are rightly loaded, a dive into your

pockets to make sure you have all you require, and off you go.

It is easy work, the spoor holds straight on ; at last it turns at right angles along a game path always through the jungle. Lions dearly love a path, and they have followed this a mile before turning off it to the right, where the trees stand closer together and grass and shrubs cover most of the red soil in every opening. Possibly some-where in here they have lain up for the day, as the sun is now up and hot, and the drops begin to gather on your brow and run down your temples. With more caution and expectation you follow on: two pair of eyes are better than one, and for lion tracking, three, provided they are good, are better still; your shikari's are mostly on the ground, your own looking ahead; your second shikari behind you uses his to confirm or to check any possible mistake, and will now and then, by a cast, put the party right when for a moment it is at fault. It goes in here and out there, round this bush and through that. The heavier weapon for close quarters is now in your hand—at any moment the grunt of a lion may announce that you are in for it. Again the country opens out a little, so that you get a view ahead, for several hundred yards at a time, and the spoor goes straight on. A touch on your arm behind and you turn to your second shikari ; his finger points ahead, he has seen something you have missed. On you go walking fast and

softly through a group of thorn trees, and there
before you is a treeless space covered with dense
flat and wide-topped khansa bush ; the track
goes right through this. Bother ! have we to
get through this too ? Bending down, you see
it is more open among the stems, and that it is
possible to work along in the thorny tunnels,
much as a pitman gets to the face of the coal in a
low seam. It is sandy and bare under the bushes,
and the track more distinct than ever. At last
you are out and glad to be erect once more.
How hot it is ! it is only ten o'clock—must not
touch my water-bottle. Wonder if my rifle-
muzzle has any sand in it. Wish my boy would
not carry that rifle with the muzzle sawing up
and down between my chest and my throat.
He pulls up dead, and so do you. " Do you see
anything ? " you whisper. " Haa," he says,
which means " yes," but signs to you not to
move ; then he slowly takes you by the sleeve
and draws you half a pace sideways. Yes, there
they both are, slouching on 200 yards in
front, in single file, apparently at a slow pace,
but really covering about four miles an hour.
In a moment they are out of sight and you hurry
on. Again a halt ; there is a shaggy-necked lion
looking at you. You can see a sort of frowning
scrutiny in his visage, but he has not made you
out to be anything worth troubling his dignity
about, for before you can step forward to get a
sight of his body he has turned and has walked

out of sight. Another long tramp on the trail, and again you see them, both together this time, standing stock-still, no movement save in the last joints of their tails, glaring at you from under a tree only 60 yards away. You take aim, but tree and lion seem all one. The lion steps out towards you, his tail lashing; he gives a grunt that shakes the ground. The big gun answers with a loud report. A streak of blood on the shoulder as he gives to the shot, and bang again as they both bound away. Run now, whilst reloading, your boy at your elbow. There they are: the wounded one has stopped, his tail is going again, and he is growling. "Pingo" goes your rifle, and he is down. Another cartridge is stuffed in, and you run forward round a bush, and from 20 yards you give him another, and he is yours. Yes, but there is the lioness too, with her eyes flashing fire, fixed on you; up goes her tail. Shoot quick—"crack" and over she rolls. Excitement makes you fire again in haste, and you shoot over her, and she is into that bush with a bound. "She is in there," your shikari is saying; "there! there! Shoot 'im! shoot 'im!" He sees her, why cannot you? He tugs you a pace forward and, crouching, points again. Yes, there she is—is it her head? Yes. "Bang"—silence. Cautiously you draw near and see that she is dead. Your boy reaches her tail very gingerly, gets hold of it and gives it a tug—she is dead as mutton. Out with her—skinning—water-bottle—lunch—and back in triumph to camp.

This day differs from every other day—all days after lions do, not only in their successes and failures, but in all the experiences of the pursuit and the behaviour of the game. Lions, when conscious that they are being followed, can be very nasty, but more often flee before you. At times you track the livelong day without their halting. One man I knew of, tracked a lion for two days; the second day he lost him on the rocks of the Gan Libah (*i.e.* the Lion's Paw, one of the Golis mountains), after a twenty-five-mile walk on his trail. This, like every lion or salmon or stag which one loses, is the finest that was ever seen. On some days you may have to call in the aid of your pony, on another he may spoil your sport. It is a good thing to get bored and tired with the whole business if you are of an excitable nature, you are less likely to get flustered when a lion adopts the plan of trying to alarm you with a horrid noise and threatening gestures; this behaviour is often mere bluff, but you can never be sure what it means. Many persons have the luck to surprise lions lying in gullies or in dry river beds, where they can be stalked and shot without much more danger than a stag; others get shots at them across rivers or ravines, but such has not been my good fortune, and I advise no one to count on getting such chances.

CHAPTER XV

HUNTING WITH DOGS AND HUNTING WITH HORSES

In following lions on foot, it saves much trouble, time, and risk to have dogs, if the right sort are obtainable, but it is a different kind of diversion and not quite so "high class" as dealing with them unaided. A good lion dog may be of any description almost, but the majority of every description are of little use for the purpose. I have seen all sorts of terriers and mongrels which were just what were wanted, dogs which would mark a lion's lair in a bush and tell you at once if he was at home, and would soon bring him to bay if he bolted, dancing and yapping round when he attempted to move, till the lion, after several attempts perhaps to blot out his diminutive assailant, would give up grunting, rushing, and dashing at him, and stand or lie facing the baying dog with an expression of disgust on his scowling countenance. The beauty of cornering a lion with dogs is that you are often quite safe to shoot at him from a distance without his attempting to charge, or to move his ground much; of course, if you approach

too near, he may possibly forget all about the
dogs and go for you like a flash. At such moments
nothing but dogs which will go in and almost or
really tackle him are of much use, and they
stand every chance of being killed at once.
These occasions are, however, not the ones when
you repeat, "Better a live dog than a dead lion."

HUNTING LIONS WITH HORSES

For real fun it is difficult, as far as African
sport is concerned, to beat hunting lions on
horseback. It can be done alone, but is much
more amusing in the company of one or two
friends, and it is a diversion in which ladies can
share the excitement whilst avoiding serious
risks. Though a pony may often come in very
usefully in other places, it is really in open
country and on plains that the best opportunities
occur for hunting lions with horses. To be out
before sunrise and to view lions leaving their kill
on the plains, to draw isolated bushes or dongas
in open country in the daytime, or to drive out
covers on the edges of prairies, or high grass
patches and reed beds known to harbour lions,
affords a great deal of sport. Blank days you
probably have, but cheetahs, hyænas, wild dogs,
wart-hogs, and even jackal and serval, are almost
always there to give you a good gallop and to
keep your eye in—in fact, you have all the glorious
uncertainty of fox-hunting.

Let me try and outline a day with the reader on the Athi Plains. In the grey dawn we have heard the distant roar of lions, and are out of bed, hurrying up the sleepy boys to get our breakfast ready, and the ponies fed and saddled. My own toilet on hunting days is a speedy affair, for my rule in Africa is to have my hot bath and a shave each night on coming in—a beard I have long discarded as too much trouble to attend to, a hot and dusty thing by day and an uncomfortable buffer between cheek and pillow at night; but every one to his own taste. Ere the snow is pink on the two peaks of Kilimanjaro we are heading for the plains. Zebra, kongoni, and gazelle stream right and left, or canter away in front of us. Now we have spread out half a mile apart, each followed by our gun-bearer, syce, and boys—we each have a light rifle in our hands. The shadows still are long, and within them, between the streams of golden light, lions and other game may escape observation. The sun gets up, and a score or two of vultures are circling fast and high far ahead. We head for this kill. Halt ! is that a lion galloping off on the right ? The binoculars say " no," only a solitary wildebeest bull with head down, mane flying and tail swirling. We draw nearer the vultures; there are large dark objects on the ground and a couple of jackal trot away across our front, stopping now and again to look at us. Yes, lions ! " Simba ! " " Mpili ! " cry the

boys. " Lions, two of them ! " and they are off at
a gallop, and so are we. They do not look as if
they were going very fast, but it takes longer
than you might expect to cover half of the mile
between them and us, though the ground is
sound, the grass short, and the ponies as keen as
mustard, for they too guess they are in for a
run. As we fly over the rolling plain, the brutes
separate. I call to you to take the right hand
one, I will take the other ; we know the game,
and a few moments bring each of us level
with our lion and some 200 yards to the
right of it.[1] We are now far from each other,
but pursue the same tactics. I forge slightly
ahead and draw a little closer on my lion, but
I am a very cautious man, and take care to
have most of 200 yards between myself and
my foe. I am now trotting, and the lioness, for
I now can see that it is one, is cantering on
with her long tail floating behind her. I know
the ground, and see she is determined to gain a
certain hollow where the grass grows coarse and
high ; she must be stopped before reaching her
refuge. I yell at her at the top of my voice :
" Hi ! hi ! stop, you brute ! " and she does so
to the word of command, and I pull my horse
up. She looks intently at me for a moment, and I
turn my pony, intending to have a shot, but off

---

[1] To ride dead behind a lion prolongs the pursuit, and to have
a lion on your right, unless you shoot off the left shoulder, instead
of on your left, places you at a disadvantage on a horse when you
want to shoot.

she goes again. Shouting at her, as we resume
the hunt, has no more effect; on she goes,
straight for her point. There is a nasty patch
of cracked, broken, and tufty ground no great
distance ahead, a poor place to trot over after
her, and still worse to have to gallop across if she
turns the tables, so dropping the reins into the
hook of my elbow as I canter on, I fire two shots
across her front. That "brings her to" with a
short turn, and again as I rein up she looks
hard at me. My pony is heaving and I know
I am not likely to hit her standing or charging,
and *it is* a charge, for her tail has gone up and
she is trotting towards us. In a moment she is
coming like a greyhound at us. One touch with
the heel and my pony too is stretching himself
out, and I have the best part of 200 yards start
of her; bar accidents, I am, with this pony,
safe enough; I am thinking much more of
steering my horse where the ground is bare and
sound than of the great beast behind us, but
looking round I see she has "chucked it," and
is trotting for her point once more. Round we
come again and get just ahead of her on
her right front. Again she stands, but only
lashes her tail and fixes her flashing eyes on
her novel and curious enemy. We stand stock-
still at 250 yards and simply watch her. I
mean to make her quite safe. She lies down,
her head toward me, her tail going now and
again. It seems a long time before my gun-

bearer and syce appear, but they have come fast
on my tracks and kept me always in view. As
they come up I draw back another 40 yards or
so, for I am very cautious. Dismounting, I
send my pony yet farther back, but not far to
the rear, for if she bolts again I shall want him.
I take my big gun, look to see that the cartridges
are right—two solid soft-lead balls; I feel in my
pockets to see that my reserve is handy, then,
placing the big gun by me on the ground, I take
the ·256 rifle, sit down and fire a shot at her
scarcely visible head. "Over" her! I give my
lyman half a turn down and shoot again. "A hit!"
she is up! "Crack" again, and she is on her
back, growling and snarling and worrying her own
leg. I take the 10-bore and go forward quickly,
and at 40 yards give her one more, and it is all over.

My pony is at my side; I am on to him
at once and off to find you. Over that far
ridge I go and scan the great plain; in the
quivering atmosphere I cannot make you out.
With my glass I see in the heated air a shivering,
streaky object—is it kongoni? No, it is too
tall; it must be you. I gallop another mile
and look again with the glass; it *is* you, and there
is your gun-bearer nearing you; you are sitting
on your pony looking at something, and I hurry
on to join you; you are in a bare place between
two small patches of high grass. As I ride up
you point to one of these; " I have got him in
here," you say, without taking your eyes off

the grass. It is not a pretty place to walk into, what shall we do? You suggest that we wait for our big guns, and then walk in together, but I say "No," being a very cautious man; "when you get your rifle, keep my boy and my big gun with you, I will go off there at right angles and fire into the grass from my pony; if he comes for me, you will get a broadside shot at him, and I can get away." I know the probabilities are that he will fear to charge either of us, for a lion attacked from different quarters does not like the idea of exposing himself to one party whilst attacking another. I go to my position and fire a shot into the grass—no movement or sound; another shot—nothing stirs; another shot—and a hideous grunt as he jumps up. There he is for a moment with his head to me and his tail lashing; a magnificent brute he looks at his last stand, with his shaggy yellow mane and his black-tipped ears set hard back amongst it. " Crack-thug " goes your rifle and he is down in a heap; he was half turned from you, and your bullet struck him in the ribs and raked forward and across him, through heart and lungs and crashed into his shoulder, splintering it to pieces. In a minute we are looking at the green light in his dead eye, and the last feeble slow and unconscious inspiration ere he sets those cruel teeth for ever. Two lions to skin, a warm job in the hot sun, but there is all the afternoon before us, and our lunch, water-bottles, and tobacco to help us

through the work. The heads and feet can be
done at leisure in the shade at home before
sundown ; in two hours' time we are well on our
way back to camp.

There is another way in which horses may be
utilized for lion-hunting, and that is the Somali
method, where you leave it to these sporting
natives to find, ride up, and hold the lions at bay
till they send for you. I know of one or two
Somali hunters who do this well in bush country,
and it is an exciting enough moment when you
arrive to deal finally with a maddened and
baited lion.

In Abyssinia I met a Count Wickenberg, who
had adopted yet another mode of riding down
lions, but a method which I think he would no
longer recommend ; it is one that I certainly
have never had the courage to attempt. He
literally rode his lions down as if they had been
pigs, and when close on the top of them shot
them with his ·256 Mannlicher. For a few weeks
he amused himself thus on the Somali Plains.
After some glorious fun and killing about a
dozen in this simple manner, one took a seat
beside him on his pony and spoilt the show.
What he went through on this occasion put him
a little out of conceit with his own system—at
least this was the impression he gave me when
he related to me the experience, and I do not
think that he or any one else has since put it
into practice.

CHAPTER XVI

NIGHT-SHOOTING

So much has been written about night-shooting, whether sitting in zaribas on the ground, or on machâns in trees, over kills, live bait, or water-pools, that I shall say little about it.[1] It is worth while trying night-shooting a few times, whether you are successful or not; the experience is interesting, and you gain a personal acquaintance with the night habits of the beasts of the forest and wilderness, as well as with the sounds and noises of African nights in the jungle and bush, from dark to dawn. From the point of view of sport only, there is, for me, too much patience and tediousness about it. Yet on occasion you may have all the excitement that is good for you, especially after daybreak, when you have to follow up a wounded lion before breakfast, after a disturbed night's rest. The whole pleasure of a night vigil in the bush is spoilt for

---

[1] In North Africa many of the lions were shot at night from a *melbeda* (ambush) or from a *zoubia* (ditch). A favourite plan was to dig a hole in the ground near a kill, or with live bait tethered close to it, and to cover this with a heavy cart-wheel. From this protected ambush the night-hunter could shoot with safety and was well hidden.

me when you sit over a live bait, whether it
be camel, cow, donkey, or goat. The vicarious
sacrifice may be justifiable on occasion, but I
abandoned live bait after a very few trials of
it. To wait hour after hour watching an animal
tethered close to you, with your thoughts anticipating its horrid end, is not pleasure—nor is
it anything but very disgusting when a hyæna
has rushed in and disembowelled the victim
under your nose. I have brained several hyænas
at their rush in, when waiting for lions, but
never killed one before he had ripped open the
animal, when I have been trying to protect live
bait. If you do not kill, and only wound a lion
at night, following the spoor in the morning
reminds me of playing, when we were children,
a game we called " Lions and Tigers," when half
the party were lions and the other half tigers.
The opposing forces take turns, say, the lions hide,
the tigers go in search ; a lion may at any moment
dash out on you with a howl, and if you are
caught before reaching home you are dead and
done for. A game to be played after dark in a
big house. Oh, delightful sensations of terror
and of being paralysed therewith !—of hair-
breadth escapes !—of realizing that you were a
dead tiger !—of relief on escaping to the refuge
out of reach of those awful claws and jaws !
All these were ours. The child is father of the
man : and many a sportsman, knowing that a
wounded lion lay hid somewhere in the thorns

and grass when they sparkled in the dawn of a Somali day, has felt once more some of these delicious sensations of childhood's days, which few things in life can give him now, as he steals on tip-toe round the trees and peers into the dark recesses of each bush.

That night-shooting may have its risks and adventures, the following story tells. My wife and I were in Somaliland at the time, but I give the story in the words of one who was a principal in the adventure, and as it appeared, I think, in the *Field*.

The following letter was written from " Camp near Shigar, Baltista, Balistan, 20th April 1896":—

" The following occurrence, which happened a few weeks ago in Somaliland, may perhaps be of interest :—

" I had for some days been trying to shoot zebra, but owing to the density of the jungle, I found it would be impossible to get a shot in the daytime. I therefore decided to sit up one night in a zariba, close to a pool where they often came to drink. That zebra were very plentiful here, at Habedleh, was not doubtful. Every day I saw any amount of tracks, and at night they kept up a constant neighing all round our camp. Accordingly one evening found Hassan and Faro, my two shikaris, and myself in a small zariba in a river bed a few yards away from the pool.

Mrs. Renton accompanied us. The zariba, just large enough to allow us four to lie down side by side, was about 8 feet high, and built extremely thick with strong thorny branches. As early as 5.30 we were shut up inside, as the zebra, if they came at all, would probably come while it was still dusk. The zariba was constructed with three loopholes. Mrs. Renton lay down under the third from the right, I was under the second, while Hassan and Faro watched alternately from the third. No zebra put in an appearance, and, leaving one shikari to keep watch in case any animal should come to drink, the remainder of us were soon sleeping as one only sleeps in the open.

" Shortly after ten I was awakened by cries of terror from Hassan. He was distractedly calling ' Faro ! Faro ! ' and I saw that there were only three of us in the zariba. A lion had carried off Faro. The night was very dark, and rain was falling. It was impossible for us to get out of the zariba, and we could see nothing outside. We were powerless to render any help to the poor man. All we could do was to keep firing into the air in the hope that the noise would frighten the lion away from his unfortunate victim, and to alarm the camp some two miles distant.

" Having heard the continued firing, some men came down from the camp in about three-quarters of an hour. They released us, and searching cautiously about we found the body. The head had a fearful bite as well as the shoulder, from which the lion had sucked the blood. We then had a difficult and gruesome march back to camp. It is no easy matter to carry a corpse along an exceedingly rocky river-bed, and it took us an hour to arrive home. This long walk was excessively trying for Mrs. Renton, after the awful ordeal she had passed through. On inspecting the zariba the following morning we found blood inside. The branches were hardly disturbed, and the loophole at which Faro had been watching—for he was actually on watch when seized—was intact. From his pugs we saw the lion had passed the first two loopholes under which Mrs. Renton and myself had been sleeping, before attacking the zariba. After dragging the unlucky man a short distance and drinking the blood, he had departed, and lain down 50 yards away. How this lion got Faro out of the zariba, I am utterly unable to explain.

" The stony nature of the ground rendered tracking the brute up impossible, and I was unfortunately obliged to leave Habedleh without closing accounts with him. A similar accident has never been known in Somaliland.

(Signed) " LESLIE RENTON."

I once sat through a long, hot, black night in a lion zariba in Somaliland, when the last thing

I had seen against the sky in the fading light was a pair of long whip snakes above my head, wriggling among the thorns of my shelter. From time to time a great lion padded round and round me within a few feet of where I sat, so near at times that I could hear him sigh. He came first while there was still a moon, but not till it was inky dark, about one o'clock in the morning, did he venture to the dead camel he had slain; then I mortally wounded him at the muzzle of my gun as I heard him tearing the flesh.

But the most uncomfortable night watch I ever kept was a mile from camp, when I had seated myself at dusk, with my shikari, under a dry river bank, with a feeble screen of two or three small thorn branches in front of me, near a water hole, round which leopard tracks were fresh. We had a white goat with us, tethered, which was to attract the leopards by its bleating, but it did not bleat, and as one of our boys said, "I can't row, I can't shoot," which being interpreted meant, "If a goat will not make a row, what chance is there of getting a shot." The hot night was still as death—seven o'clock, eight o'clock passed slowly by, and then I heard something walking on the bank behind us with long, slow, lurching steps. I held my breath as it approached, and my shikari, crouching at my side, whispered "Libah!" (lion). It passed, but from that moment I was on edge. A lion about, and he had passed within three yards of my head; he might drop down from above or rush us from in front. We heard hyænas' ghoulish howls between intervals of silence, and then animals drinking at the pool hidden in the blackness 60 yards in front of us; we heard also the lion or lions drinking there, and then something heavy walk past us up the bed of the river. Half an hour of this was as much as my nerves could stand, or rather, the idea of eight or nine more hours of it was. I said to my boy, " We will go back to camp." " Not safe, sahib," said he. I replied, " Safe or not safe, I am going; light the lantern, take it and lead the way." I had no stomach for sitting there like my poor goat, which stood quietly staring into the blackness, awaiting its end. It was pitch dark, the candle only seemed to make the night blacker. I stood with the gun while the goat was untethered, and off started my shikari, lantern in one hand and leading the goat with the other. I followed with gun full-cock, feeling very unprotected behind as we passed the pool and stumbled along the river bed. Then it struck us that it would be safer in the bush beyond the banks, so we scrambled up the bank and into the jungle, a most horrid walk, and the mile seemed like four. When I reached camp it was not ten o'clock, and I was mighty pleased to be within the zariba.

In many parts of Africa, shouting and a

lighted lantern, or even striking matches, is a
fairly adequate defence from lions when out in
the dark, but not so in Somaliland, where these
beasts are accustomed nightly to native noise,
fires, and flaring brands. Many of them care
little enough for voice or flame, and I want no
more sitting out at night without the protection
of a strong zariba.

I have done no night-shooting by flashlight,
blue lights, nor with acetylene lamps, and to
those who have used these methods I must leave
it to describe the results. It is, I understand,
often a very successful and interesting way of
seeing and slaying lions and other nocturnal
prowlers. What the night watcher may see is
beautifully illustrated in such recent works as
those by Schilling and Dugmore.

LASSOING LIONS

This extraordinary feat has been performed
in British East Africa by Buffalo Jones and a
party of American cowboys, who brought over
their horses from the States for the purpose.
They astonished the world with what they
accomplished, for not only did they rope a lioness,
but a very large rhinoceros, as well as other
game, such as giraffe, eland, zebra, cheetah, etc.

CHAPTER XVII

HINTS FOR BEGINNERS

THE following hints for would-be lion hunters on horseback may assist them to reduce the danger of the sport to a reasonable minimum. All danger cannot be avoided ; were it possible, you might as well content yourself with traps and poison, but what is wanted is a respectable amount and not a surfeit. When all has been said and every precaution taken, there will still remain the risk of your horse falling with you over treacherous ground, the possible miscarriage of your tactics when a lion is after you, the chances of a mistake in judgment, a hesitation in resolution, the misfire or jam of a cartridge— in fact, a dozen things may happen, not to mention that you may, on occasion, be called on to attempt to save a friend, or your boys, from peril.

1. Thoroughly overhaul rifles and ammunition before starting. Take clean, fresh cartridges, and see that your supply is sufficient for yourself, your saddle-bags, and gun-bearers.

2. Remember, whenever it is practicable, to keep on the off, *i.e.* the right, side of any lion

you ride after, unless you shoot from the left shoulder. Tactics do not always allow of this, but it is a point to bear in mind.

3. Never lose sight of your lion for a second, if you can help it, for while you turn your head he may squat and leave you an empty plain to stare at. If he " claps," keep your eye glued to the very spot where he has gone down.

4. When mounted, never approach within 100 yards of a lion — 150 yards is a safer distance.

5. When you are alone, never dismount within 200 yards of a lion, unless you are absolutely sure that your pony will allow you to mount the moment you wish to, and that he will stand perfectly still, without his reins being on the ground, while you are on your feet.

6. If you are off your horse and find a lion is within 100 yards of you, do not attempt to mount ; if he looks like charging, take your shot carefully and quickly ; if he has started, wait till he is at 25 yards before firing your first barrel. Remember a large proportion of accidents are due to the failure to realize, before it has been seen, the velocity of a lion's charge. The best way to obtain an idea of it is to place yourself for a moment in front of a motor - car coming straight at you, 100 yards off, going at a speed of, say, 40 miles an hour, and see how much time it would leave you for mounting or for doing anything more than

putting up your rifle and placing a bullet in it. Never shoot at an advancing lion with your reins hooked over your arm, in your hand, or even under your foot. The steadiest pony in the world may flinch and wince at the sight of a lion crashing down on him.

7. Never follow a lion, when you are alone, into high grass, whether you are mounted or not. Two rifles following a lion into grass or covert should keep near each other, but not elbow to elbow. If he attacks one and there is some five yards or more separating the rifles, the other rifle gets a larger and more vital target to shoot at, and the chance is increased of success in stopping him if the first rifle fails or has not time to fire.

8. If through an accident you are caught, do not give up hope. A knife has saved a man's life, and I have never been without boys with me whom I could not trust to make an effort to save me in a tight place. Remember a lion will sometimes go off and leave his victim of his own accord. Swayne recommends a double-barrelled 12-bore pistol in the belt.

9. Always have antiseptics and bandages with you. Remember that much more than half the accidents with lions, which terminate fatally, are only fatal through blood-poisoning. The neglect of very simple precautions promptly applied has often led to fatal results. The man who is tempted to mistrust his own nerve should

recollect that men's nerves do not fail them when a lion charges; there is no time at that moment to be afraid; it is all over in a second or so, and the bravest thing he could do would be to turn tail and deliberately throw away his last chance. The meanest of God's creatures will, when cornered, often put up a splendid fight against heavy odds, and man has not yet become the meanest of these. I have seen men reckless, foolhardy, or excited and wild, but never a single one whose nerve forsook him when once in for a battle with a lion : it goes without saying that there are occasions when discretion is the better part of valour.

APPENDIX I

THE LION IN ANCIENT HISTORY

AMONG many of the nations of Europe, Asia, and Africa, the lion in ancient times was raised to the position of a divinity. He was often worshipped as a god or venerated as a sacred creature, and he was to the fore in the earliest collections of tamed and untamed wild beasts. He became the companion of not a few emperors and kings. He was trained to fight in battles and to pursue and kill game for his masters. The lion's rôle in past ages may be studied in Gustave Loisel's exhaustive works, *Histoire des Ménageries de l'Antiquité à nos jours* (3 vols.). The first volume is a most interesting and fascinating one, and from it nearly all the following facts are taken. Loisel cites fully the sources from which he has gained his information, and the Bibliographical Index (at the end of his first volume) is by itself of great value.

In Egypt lions were worshipped at Leontopolis and Heliopolis. At Heliopolis the sacred lion lived in the Temple of the Sun (Ammon Ra); his food was most carefully selected, and sacred melodies were played to him during his meals.

The Egyptians not only tamed, but trained, wild beasts to an extent and with a thoroughness that must appear to us very remarkable. Wild cats, cheetahs, leopards, striped hyænas, wild dogs (*Lycaon*), and lions were all trained for the chase.

After the XIIth Dynasty (or between 3000 and 2000 B.C.) we no longer find *Hyæna* and *Lycaon* used for hunting, but between 1700 and 100 B.C., after the

XVIIIth and XIXth Dynasties, the lions and cheetahs continue to be used in the packs of hunting-beasts. In Egypt, as in Assyria, the lions were usually shaved, and were also used in war. Rameses ii. (XIXth Dynasty) was accompanied to battle by his lion Anta-m-nekht, who went in front of his chariot alongside the horses and struck down with a blow of his paw any one who came near.

Up to the time of the Roman occupation of Egypt any man who could afford to possess lions was allowed to have them. After the Theban period, under the Ptolemies and at Alexandria, lions were still used in religious festivals and in the processions to celebrate victories. One such procession under Ptolemy vi. Philometor consisted of a series of enormous sections each devoted to the honour of one of the divinities.

In the section devoted to Dionysus (Bacchus), following the numerous groups of satyrs and sileni there came a car drawn by eighty men, on which was borne the statue of Bacchus, and which was surrounded by priests and priestesses, after which came many more cars and followers, and then came the wild beasts. The menagerie animals were led by an elephant guided by a little satyr sitting astride on the elephant's neck ; then came 500 young girls, then 24 cars drawn by elephants, 60 cars drawn by oxen, 12 cars drawn by lions, with many more following drawn by wild asses, ostriches, stags, and other beasts. Near the end of the procession we find 1 great white bear, 14 leopards, 16 panthers, 4 lynx, 3 little bears, 1 giraffe, and 1 rhinoceros.

After the Roman Conquest the sacred menageries were allowed to continue till about 384 A.D., when the Emperor Theodosius abolished the worship of animal-gods and began the destruction of the temples.

However, farther up the Nile, the cults of Isis and Osiris continued at such places as Philæ until Justinian put an end to them in the sixth century.

King hunting Lions.

Our information with regard to the collections of animals amongst the ancient Chinese is not so full, but they existed. Marco Polo saw with amazement in 1271 lions and tigers strolling quite free in the apartments of the Palace of Cabalut (the modern Pekin). Lions, leopards, and other beasts were trained also for the chase.

In *India* various animals and reptiles besides the cow and the bull were held sacred. In the first century of our era, lions, panthers, and cheetahs were trained to hunt, and were so domesticated as to be given entire liberty about the palaces and gardens.

Our knowledge with regard to *Assyria* and *Chaldea*

Wounded Lioness.

reaches much further back into the past. Six centuries before the time of Moses we find the lion numbered among the animal-gods of Babylon.

In the Assyrian Galleries of the British Museum some most graphic sculptures and bas-reliefs may be seen in which the lion appears. Those from the Palace of Sardinapalis are particularly interesting. These Assyrian lions were shaved when domesticated. Of the mane only a frill or collar was left round the face; on the body some tufts and bands of hair were left on the back, along the flanks, and behind the thighs. The tuft was left at the end of the tail. This seems to be the probable origin of the fashion in shaving poodles.

[*Photo, Mansell.*

LIONS LET OUT OF CAGE.

From Slab in British Museum.

[*Photo, Mansell.*

ASSUR-BANI-PAL ON HORSEBACK SPEARING LION.

To face p. 262.

The lion was also among the animals venerated and held sacred by the *Persians*. In the temples of the Goddess Anahita the lions were so tame that they caressed visitors to her shrine in the most friendly manner, and behaved with " modesty and decency " at their meals. In the spectacular combats provided by the Persian kings we find lions matched against bulls. Alexander the Great made lions fight against dogs and sometimes against men for his entertainment, but he also kept lions in his palace.

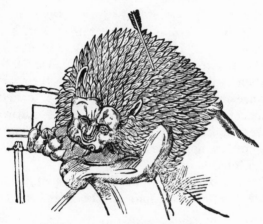

Lion seizing Chariot Wheels.

In Persia it was the custom to preserve large numbers of wild animals in great game parks, where they were hunted; lions were included in the game with which these parks were stocked.

From the East, from the Euphrates, and from the Nile the cult of wild beasts spread to Carthage and the West. The *Phœnicians* included the lion among the animals they regarded as sacred.

The *Greeks* never had the extensive menageries that were found in the precincts of Egyptian temples. The Greeks preferred less ferocious animals or birds. But the priests of Artemis fed certain wild beasts, and probably held them more or less sacred. In Asia Minor lions and leopards were kept in the temples of Cybele (Rhea and Idæa are among the other names by which this goddess is known ; she was called by the Romans Ops, and known as " Magna Mater," and regarded by them as the representative of plenty).

Virgil thus refers to Cybele and her lions : " Hinc mater cultrix Cybeli Corybantiaque aera Idaeumque nemus, hinc fida silentia sacris, et juncti currum dominae subiere leones."—ÆNEID, Book iii.

In Greece the priests of Cybele were mendicant friars who were accompaned by tamed wild beasts in their wanderings. Lions were used by them as exorcists. Later the Agyrtes (begging monks) passed on into Italy with their wild beasts. They found their lions in abundance in the Greek mountains. Up to and after the time of Aristotle, even in the third century B.C., lions were found on the mountains of Pongæus and Pindus, in the north-west of Macedonia, on Olympus, and in Ætolia.

After the battle of Pharsalia, the people of Megaris let loose a number of lions on the Romans who were besieging them.

The first appearances in Italy of lions, bears, and leopards in religious association with the cult of Isis, Cybele, and Bacchus, seems to have been on the advent of the wandering monks from Greece.

In the third century before Christ, the Romans first began to have large collections of wild beasts, and to make use of elephants in war.

About the year 185 B.C., Marcus Fulvius Nobilior, having returned from his campaign in Greece, introduced the hunting and killing of lions in the amphitheatre. Until 146 B.C., the public spectacle of butcheries of prisoners and deserters in the arena, by trampling them to death with elephants or giving them to wild beasts, was only occasional, but the custom soon spread after this time through all Italy.[1]

Sylla, after receiving lions as a present from Bochus, King of Mauritania, provided 100 male lions to be hunted to death in the arena.

Pompey put into the arena at one time 600 lions and lionesses and 18 or 20 elephants, and also the first rhinoceros ever seen in Rome. Julius Cæsar gave 400 lions and the first giraffe ever seen by the Romans for one of these spectacles. These butcheries became more frequent under the emperors. The following are the numbers of the lions found in some of the later Roman imperial menageries :—

Octavius Augustus (29 to 14 B.C.), 260 lions.

Nero (54–68 A.D.), 300 lions.

Antoninus (138–161 A.D.), 100 lions.

Commodus (180–193 A.D.), 100 lions.

Caracalla (211–217 A.D.) had a favourite lion named Acinaces, which he kept at his side when at table and in his bedroom.

Heliogabalus (218–222).—Loisel recounts the pranks played by this emperor on his boon companions with lions and other beasts whom he had mutilated and deprived of their teeth and claws.

Probus (276–282) possessed 100 maned lions and 100 lionesses.

---

[1] Pliny (*see* Holland's *Pliny*, 1601 edition) asserts that Q. Scævola, son of Publius, was the first that in his Curule Ædileship exhibited a fight and combat of many lions together; that L. Sylla when " Pretor represented a shew of an hundred Lions with manes and collars of haire "; that Pompeius the Great showed 600 of them fighting in the Grand Cirque, whereof 315 were male lions with manes; and that Cæsar Dictatour brought 400 of them into the "Shew place." Many quaint bits of translation will be found in Holland's *Pliny*, *e.g.*: " If he (*i.e.* the lion) chaunce to be wounded hee hath a marveilous eye to marke the partie that did it, and be the hunters never so many in number, upon him he runneth onely."

During the Roman period trained lions were by no means unknown.

For the whole history of menageries, and for descriptions of existing collections of wild animals, zoological gardens, and game parks, the reader is referred to Loisel's volumes referred to above.

APPENDIX II

RIFLES AND PROJECTILES FOR DANGEROUS GAME

FOR those interested in the behaviour of bullets and who require guidance with regard to the choice of weapons, I give a letter written by myself to the *Field*, May 13, 1911, and the comments and criticism thereon by the Hon. T. F. Fremantle, who is the best authority I know on the practical and theoretical bearings of the subject.

THE BEST ALL-ROUND RIFLE

SIR,—The letter of " Garhwali " in the *Field*, 22nd April, is excellent, and deserves the attention of all big game hunters. I desire to obtain the assistance of those better qualified than I am to demonstrate scientifically the soundness or otherwise of the conclusions I have arrived at from experience and observation in regard to one particular phase of the important question " Garhwali " has raised. I am persuaded that unless the shortcomings of the ·280 Ross and other small-bore rifles are exposed and brought home to rifle-makers as well as to hunters, that many valuable lives will be sacrificed by those who, like my friend the late Mr. George Grey, had faith in their all-round superiority over other weapons, even for such dangerous game as lions. For eighteen years I have stuck to the ·256 Mannlicher for general purposes, and consider it " good enough," and especially convenient for shooting from horseback. I have never advocated rifles of this class for close quarters with lions, and, though I have killed many lions with the ·256, I have killed most of them at long range, and generally with a 10-bore held in reserve. I consider that ·400 is the smallest bore modern rifle suitable for dangerous game at close quarters. I do not agree with " Garhwali " that a single-shot rifle is preferable to a magazine rifle : I think for dangerous game at close quarters a double-barrelled one is infinitely preferable. I have in the last three months thrice seen the single-barrelled rifle jam when face to face with dangerous game, all high-class rifles (Rigby ·450, Lancaster ·450, and Jeffery ·404). I do not know of a single-shot rifle where there is not the liability of an empty case refusing to be extracted ; I have never experienced the refusal of a cartridge to be extracted from a magazine rifle, though these rifles may go wrong in other ways at a critical moment.

The point I want to make in this letter is that cordite or nitro powders and modern projectiles, in a rifle however powerful, give no advantage with a charging lion at close quarters over old-fashioned 8-, 10- or 12-bore rifles and guns with a big charge of powder and solid lead ball. By close quarters I mean within 25 yards from a charging lion which is covering 100 yards in three seconds. Before entering on the question of weapons, I should like to give my view of what the conditions are which the weapon is required for in the case of lions only. In my opinion the lion has many attributes that differentiate it from all other classes of dangerous African game. Only the leopard attacks with the same lightning, or even greater rapidity, but the inferior weight, size, strength, and armament of the leopard puts him into a totally different category. He can be dealt with with a shot gun. Many men seized or attacked by leopards have killed them with their bare hands. I have known two instances of this myself.

The "knock-out" target presented by a lion at, say, 60 yards when charging on the level is very small. A head shot above the level of the eyes is liable to glance. A lion coursing towards the shooter is very likely to be shot over, as his pace is generally very great.

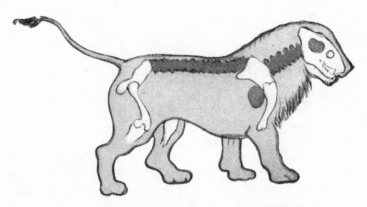

Diagram to show how much of a lion's broadside presents a "knock-out" target. A shot to stop a charging lion must be in the brain, neck, or spine. A shot in the heart within 60 yards is not to be relied on.

To face p. 268.

The lion when he charges is coming faster than a greyhound. I do not know what the momentum or striking energy of a lion (apart from muscular striking power) would be, but this can be calculated on the basis of, say, 300 lb. to 400 lb. travelling sixty miles an hour. But no rifle projectile will give an equivalent striking energy to the lion's. For practical purposes, the striking energy figures given for rifles by gunmakers are entirely misleading. A lion is not a steel target. I am not good at figures, but I calculate that a 1-oz. ball travelling 2000 ft. per second has a striking momentum at least twenty-eight times too little to counteract and bring to rest the charging momentum of a 400 lb. lion, if the lion had an impenetrable hide and could get it all—all at once and in one place. But no rifle or gun could or need do anything of this sort. To be efficient, it must be the most capable weapon for instantaneously killing or paralysing a living creature carrying 200 lb. to 400 lb. at the rate of 100 ft. per second towards you, with added forces of limbs, teeth, and claws. In gunmaker's lingo, what is required is " shock " ; that term is applicable to the desideratum for all other dangerous African game, but the only certainly effective shock to a charging lion is a bullet in the brain or vertebral column.

No man can make sure of giving this shot. The bead drawn on the head of a charging lion with cool deliberation is only done in imagination and in dreams or in fiction. A shot in the brain or spinal column must always be a fluke, and almost any rifle can do that work. As no man without a moment's warning can make sure of hitting a charging lion in the brain, and is unlikely to have any of the vertebral column in sight, and in all probability never sees anything of a lion's head above the eyes, and could no more draw a bead on it than if it was a snipe, and if he could would most certainly miss the spot aimed at, all we can hope to obtain is the knowledge of what weapon and what projectile gives a man the best chance of knocking out a charging lion.

Lion charges occur sometimes with warning, often without any. The man who has time to anticipate a charge can do certain things. He may have time to step behind a tree or bush, or to sit down or kneel to shoot. As far as position is concerned, the sitting position, though less suited for quick work, and for giving command of the situation, may give certain men greater confidence and minimize the shock of impact if the lion " gets home." Personally, I prefer the standing position ; you command a larger field and can judge pace and distance quicker. What is required in such rapid work is a weapon powerful enough to give shock (with a projectile that behaves the best in practice) and yet which can be quickly manipulated and easily handled.

The following points require attention : (1) After a lion has started on his charge, no man is likely to get in more than two shots (I have no experience of large-bore automatic weapons, but they are liable to jam) ; therefore a double-barrelled weapon is the most effective. The magazine rifle is inferior ; it is slower in manipulation, and the aim is destroyed between each shot. (2) A man is more likely to hit his mark with a weapon he is familiar with. Few men, comparatively, are really familiar with heavy rifles, and fewer still shoot as well with a heavy rifle as with a small one. All rifles smaller than ·400 are dangerous to use on charging lion. The ·400 is not too heavy a rifle to become handy with or for daily use. (3) Any double-barrelled weapon may be selected of a calibre of ·400, or larger calibre that can be easily handled ; 12-bore and 10-bore shot and ball guns answer this requirement. (4) The superiority of 12- and 10-bore weapons over heavy rifles is, in the case of lions, more marked in their projectiles than in the ease of their handling, when knock-out shots must be given within 25 yards range. It is within this range that such guns show their superiority over powerful cordite rifles.

I do not know what the muzzle velocity of a 10-bore gun, with the equivalent charge to 5 drs. of black powder and bullets of 800 grs. each may be, nor what the striking energy of such a ball at 25 yards and under is. On paper, of course, it will be very inferior to a cordite ·450 to ·500 bore rifles with 460 grs. or 500 grs. bullets, but the behaviour of the 10- and 12-bore projectiles is on the average greatly superior.

For the heavy cordite rifle two types of bullets may be used, the solid or expanding (soft-nosed, slit, etc.); but at close range you gain little value in knocking-out power, whereas with an ordinary 12-bore shot-gun, even with No. 5 shot, at 3 yards you would blow a lion's head to pieces or drive an enormous hole through his body.

The question of the projectile is of the utmost importance. All probably agree that what is required is the biggest possible blow, and the one most instantaneously destructive to muscular action. If the hard-cased bullet of the modern rifle is left solid, with its envelope intact, the result of a close range hit is to drill a small hole through the animal, and a large proportion of the intended blow may be wasted beyond the lion; and these hard-cased bullets, which have to be long in order to get the necessary weight into a small-bore projectile, are very liable to glance and deflect on contact with smooth surfaces of bone and skull (see diagram). To remedy this waste of striking power and to increase the area of injury, the expanding or soft-nosed bullet is used, which means that the envelope enclosing the lead is no longer intact. What can anyone suppose is the condition of this lead on leaving the muzzle of a rifle, after the bullet has passed with enormous friction at inconceivable pace through a rifled barrel, and issues from the muzzle at between 2000 to 3000 feet per second velocity ? It must be reduced to fluid, and fluid in an opened envelope. This is how I explain the fact that when a lion is hit in the face with one of these bullets at close range, if the bullet is not deflected it often goes to pieces and nothing is to be found of lead save faint splashes, and only a bit of light twisted metal envelope is discovered not far in, and out of the line of the original line of entry. I have twice seen charging lions hit in the face at 5 yards with such projectiles (in the nose and mouth), and in both cases the lion might just as well have been missed. Will anyone say that a solid lead bullet or even small shot from a 12-bore gun would not do better work ? It is, I believe, an old illustration, but apposite, that though the rapier may be a deadlier weapon than the fist, with greater penetration and giving greater theoretical " shock," yet if you run a man through the body with your rapier he may yet have time to run you through too, whereas if you hit him in the face with your fist you can knock him out of time and dispose of him as you will.

Given the scientific data, I have little doubt what I have found to be the result of experience, practice, and observation could be demonstrated also scientifically. The muzzle-velocity of the respective rifles is required, and subsequent velocity and momentum of each projectile at the ranges, say, of 5 yards, 25 yards, and 50 yards, in order to complete the data for argument. The size, weight, shape, and behaviour of the projectile are each points of prime importance, as well as the velocity, momentum, and penetration. A long, pointed, tapering bullet, with hard envelope, is easily deflected, no matter what its velocity. A blade of grass may alter its direction ; a touch on the branch of a tree may turn it over and tip it up or send it sideways on its journey.

It appears to me that a scientific treatment of the subject might follow the lines indicated below. The stopping power of a bullet on a charging lion depends

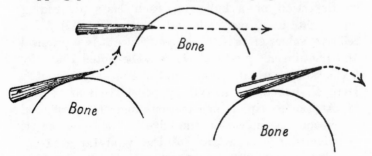

Illustrating the Path of a Long Tapering Bullet with reference to Smooth Bone.

on three principal constituents : (*a*) Area of vital target commanded by a bullet of each class. (By " vital target " is meant the target within which a bullet with adequate penetration instantaneously kills the lion or anchors him where he is.) Supposing we calculate the

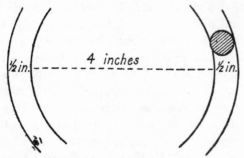

Bullet inflicting Fatal Injury.

size of this target by assuming an inner target, and its area that of a circle 4 in. in diameter $= \left(\dfrac{4}{2}\right)^{2} \times \dfrac{22}{7}$ in. $=$ $12\frac{1}{2}$ sq. in. area approximately. A bullet need only touch the circumference of this inner target to be fatal. Therefore a bullet making a $\frac{1}{2}$-in. diameter hole commands almost a 5-in. diameter vital target). (*b*) Area of injury inflicted by a bullet of each class. (*c*) Momentum (shock power) and freedom from liability to deflection of a bullet of each class (depending on weight, pace, material, and shape of bullet). The relative values of these three constituents is a physical and anatomical question. It may be noted that any bullet coming wholly (1) within the 4-in. target is fatal. Here all bullets with ordinary penetration are equal. (2) Assuming equal penetration and regularity of expansion for bullets on the edge of the 4-in. target, the increase in the area of the vital target commanded by the bullet is in direct proportion to the area of injury, since both vary in proportion to the square of half the diameter of the bullet after expansion. (3) The stopping power of any bullet is insignificant unless it goes near the vital target. (4) Bullets clear of the vital target depend for their stopping power mainly on the area of injury, and their stopping power is insignificant unless the area of injury is large. (5) A heavy bullet with low striking velocity inflicts greater proportional injury than a light bullet at high striking velocity, because it has greater bruising power, whereas the light bullet, striking at high velocity, does little injury outside the space which it actually penetrates. Thus many a man badly wounded with a ·303 bullet in action does not know at the moment that he has been shot, but if hit with a spent 7-lb. projectile is instantane-ously " floored," and might receive more conscious shock from a spent ·303 than from a bullet that passed through him. Or, to take another illustration, compare a stone thrown through a pane of glass and a bullet fired through it. The bullet may drill a small, clean hole ; the stone shatters the glass in every direction. A similar though less pronounced difference may be expected from difference in velocity of bullets striking the skull or bones of an animal. (6) The liability of a bullet to deflection depends on its weight, pace, shape, material, and the character of its expansion. The material affects either the weight or the character of its expansion or both. Moderate pace gives a heavy bullet freedom from deflection, since nothing in a lion's anatomy can resist the weight of it. Great pace gives a light bullet freedom from deflection only if the shape of the bullet and character of expansion assist. But great pace and accuracy of flight can only be got out of deeply rifled barrels, and the bullets available for these must be incased in harder metal than lead to secure the retention of shape and to enable the bullet to " take " the rifling and to obtain the spin which gives its accuracy of flight. But these bullets do not expand so evenly as plain lead bullets, and where expansion is irregular the bullet may (? will) tend to expand least in the direction in which most resistance is encountered. If this last surmise is correct, the vital organs being most protected, the expansion of cased bullets tends to be away from them. The mushrooming of pure lead balls is generally fairly even, that of soft-nosed or open cased bullets generally lobsided. A long, pointed bullet is more liable to deflection than a blunt, flat-nosed, and shorter bullet, though velocity diminishes the liability to deflection.

What I want to know is the weight of each class of bullet, its striking velocity, its average expansion in each class of rifle or gun at the ranges likely to be used with a charging lion—say, at 50 yards, 25 yards, 10 yards, and 5 yards—and apply the results to the (a) vital target, the (b) area of injury considered first in section of the cylinder of injury and then in length of cylinder of injury (penetration), and (c) probabilities of deflection or breaking up on contact. I believe in this way only can any demonstration be given of " shock," and that it could be proved that the actual momentum shock given by any rifle or gun is hardly worth taking into consideration when the question is one of stopping a charging lion and could not reduce his pace by one-fiftieth part, and would exhibit what weapon and what projectile commands best the vital target, gives the greatest area of injury, and will give the least risks of deflection or of bad behaviour.

ALFRED E. PEASE.

PINCHINTHORPE, GUISBOROUGH, YORKSHIRE.

LETTER FROM HON. T. F. FREMANTLE TO SIR ALFRED PEASE

THE OLD HOUSE, SWANBOURNE,
WINSLOW, 23/5/11.

DEAR PEASE,—Your letter in the *Field* is full of interest. I am afraid we can never find a general solution for the problem of the most effective weapon for all big game shooting. Rifles and bullets necessarily are a compromise. To get the best results in any case one should know not only what beast is to be fired at, but where the shot will hit it, and the range at which it is to be struck.

The question of stopping-power as between the old big-bore weapons such as Sir S. Baker used, and modern high velocity rifles, is a very difficult one. The older rifles were, I suppose, developed in the course of evolution from round-ball weapons the penetration of which was inadequate. By giving the ball a bigger mass, the penetration and shock were increased for big game. Sir S. Baker rightly insisted on soft-lead projectiles for such weapons; when the penetration became ample, the damaging effects from a bullet which would deform or break up could be called into play.

We have travelled further since those days, and the problem with modern rifles is to prevent the excessive penetration wasting the power of the projectile. There is, generally speaking, plenty of power. The big-bore bullet depended largely on its area for its destructiveness. The modern small-bore bullet, while penetrating at a high velocity, exerts an even greater effect ; for it communicates to the fragments of tissue and of bone which it displaces velocity enough to cause them to act as projectiles in their turn, and also produces damage by hydraulic effects on the liquids in the circulation, etc.

The first problem, I suppose, with large game, is to ensure that the bullet penetrates into the interior cavity of the body or head. A bullet reduced almost to a shell, in order to encourage expansion, will suit smaller game where the body or head cavities are not heavily overlaid with muscle or bone, but will break up, as it were, on the surface of a large animal without penetrating to vital parts. There was in the old days of the old express rifles much failure on big game— even sambur, etc.—from the failure of gunmakers to realize that the bullet which would break up inside a Scotch stag might not get inside a much heavier animal, but though it would break up, might produce only superficial injury. Selous killed the biggest game with solid bullets in the ·450 express.

The small-bore rifles suitable for antelope will, I suppose, kill a lion effectively if you can get a deliberate shot at his ribs and so put the bullet into the body cavity to do its full damage there, or if its spine can be struck from behind. But any charging animal has its body cavity and spine and brain protected by the muscles of the fore-limbs, and the bones and jaws and head, etc. You want, therefore, a bullet giving a much larger degree of penetration before breaking up than in the case of a side shot, and an antelope bullet is no good at all. The bullet will glance and break up on the face bones, as you say. In such cases it seems to me that the mass of the round bullets ensures penetration, and their larger area partly compensates for the absence of the special destructive effect which velocity adds to a projectile. In all killing, adequate penetration to meet the particular case is the first foundation of effect. With a more massive bullet than the ·303 or ·256, the base will penetrate even if the nose is broken up.

Pray put out of your mind the idea that the lead of the bullet is melted by the friction in the barrel. The primary object of the hard envelope is to prevent its being so melted ; and if it melts, the bullet will not fly true. I have known (experimental) bullets scatter a fine spray of melted lead in the air, but this difficulty is quite well understood and guarded against, and does not arise even with modern rifles giving up to 3000 ft. secs. velocity.

It is quite clear, as you indicate, that in exchanging to some extent mass for speed, as we have done in modern rifles, we have made the destructive effect rather less certain and more liable to be diverted by the accident of precisely how and where it strikes. We have *per contra* got more manageable weapons. The question of " shock " is in the case of the charging lion all-important. But we cannot expect to meet his momentum by an equal momentum on the part of the bullet. A lion weighing 400 lb. and going 60 miles an hour (but does it go twice as fast as a Derby winner ?) will have a momentum of one hundred and twenty times as much as that of a 3-ounce 4-bore bullet at 1400 f.s. The shock which turns aside a charging elephant, like that which one may read of in the old days, when the round ball flattened itself on the forehead of the buffalo, and brought him for a moment half stunned to his knees, is a shot which produces some local injury or temporary nerve damage apart from the mere question of its weight. But the local injury must go deep enough to tell.

I suppose the main moral is that one should never tackle big game without one's weapon having a big margin of destructive power.

The diminution in velocity of a h.v. bullet in 5 or 10 or 20 yards is not enough to affect materially its penetrative or destructive powers. An ordinary ·303 bullet, if starting with a velocity of 2900 f.s., will lose less than 100 f.s. in going 25 yards.

I can write only as an " arm-chair " man about dangerous game. . . .—Yours sincerely,

T. F. FREMANTLE.

SKETCH DIAGRAM

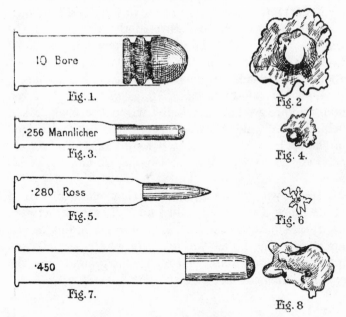

FIGS. 1, 3, 5, and 7 are outlines of cartridges.

FIG. 2, solid soft lead 10-bore ball taken out of a lion.

FIG. 4, steel and nickel enveloped ·256 soft-nosed bullet taken out of a lion.

FIG. 6, the largest fragment of a ·280 Ross bullet taken out of the lion that killed George Grey—all that was found.

FIG. 8, Rigby ·450 soft-nosed bullet taken out of a dead animal (? rhinoceros).

The preceding diagram is intended to illustrate the superiority of heavy and large projectiles on lions at close quarters over high velocity small bullets in hard envelopes. The contrast is as between a sledge-hammer blow and running an animal through with a knitting-needle. It is not intended to assert that these figures represent the normal behaviour of each projectile.

Fig. 6.—This fragment was a thin morsel of the envelope of the bullet stripped of all lead. I should think, in fact, that Fig. 2 exaggerates the average good behaviour of solid lead ball at close quarters, but taking my own experience with two unwounded lions at 5 yards range (or under) and three shots fired with soft solid lead ball.

Lion No. 1.—The ball entered the chest, went the length of the body, and three-quarters (about) of its mass was embedded in the hip joint. This lion went about 200 yards before he dropped dead.

Lion No. 2.—First barrel, 9 yards; second barrel, under 5 yards. The first ball entered the neck, raked behind the shoulder, ripped along his ribs, and lodged in the stifle, and did not stop him a bit. The second entered the neck an inch or two higher and broke his neck.

Again with a wounded lion that charged. At 5 yards range a hardened solid lead ball entered between his eyes, smashed his skull, and blew his brains out at his neck. The bullet was scarcely at all altered from its original form, and rolled on to the ground from the exit hole in the neck (see Fig. 9).

Fig. 9.

APPENDIX III

SOME NAMES FOR THE LION IN AFRICA

LANGUAGE.	NAMES.
Acholi .	. Labuor.
Aluru .	. Umboro.
Amoxosa	. Ingonyama.
Arabic .	. Sba, Asad, Sab, Sabu, Sibaa.

These are the commoner names in Arabic for lion in North Africa.[1] The Arabic name is found corrupted in various native languages, *e.g.* Swahili, Kavirondo, Jalno, etc.

Arukaya	. Kami.
Ba .	. Kemi.
Bari .	. Kamiru.
Basuto.	. Tau.
Bechuana	. Tau.
Boer (Dutch)	Leeuw.
Dinka .	. Dud.
Dorobo	. Netundo.
Dutch .	. Leeuw.
Hausa .	. Zaki.
Herero.	. O-ngeama.
Hottentot	. Gamma.
Jalno .	. Sibur.
Kamasia	. Getundo.
Kanuri	. Bundi.
Karamojo	. Enatuny.
Kavirondo	. Siburr.
Kikamba	. Munyambo or Mwenyambo.

---

[1] In Algeria I have found the words *Saïd, Houche,* and *Metelouf* used for lion. It is said that there are nearly 700 names or terms used for the lion in Arabic dialects and literature.

Language.	Names.
Kikuyu	Morodi or Ngatia.
Kitaita	Shimba.
Logwari	Kemi.
Luganda	Mpologama or Mporogama
Lukonde	Linu.
Lungo	Nu.
Lunyara	Linani.
Lusinga	Endui.
Lusoga	Mpologama or Mporogama.
Lusokwai	Linu.
Luwonga	Linani.
Madi	Ebi.
Masai	Ol-ngatuny.
Mashangama	Ibulibesi.
Matabele names	Isilwane or Impamvu or Ingwonyama.
Matonga	Ibulubesi.
Mogodo	Sungai.
Mundu	Kemi.
Nandi	Gatun.
Ngisu	Ol-natuin.
Nyam-Nyam	Mbanbono or Mbanguru.
Ogiek	Ngatundo.
Olukonjo	Endare.
Oruhima	Entare.
Ruanda	Entare.
Somali	Libah { ar, male lion; -arki, the lion. / gol, lioness; -golshi, the lioness.
Suk	Notuny.
Swahili	Simba.
Swazi	Ingonyama or Imbube or Imbubesi.
Turkana	Enatuny.
Turkish	Aslan.
Urutoro	Ekicuncu.
Zambesi Natives	Nkango.
Zulu	Ingonyama or Imbube or Imbubesi.

APPENDIX IV

ADDENDUM TO CHAPTER VII., *RE* LIONS IN BRITISH EAST AFRICA

WHILST this book was in the press, Mr. L. J. Tarlton of Nairobi most kindly supplied me with the following information, in reply to some questions I addressed to him :—

" *Lions killed in East Africa and Uganda.*—The only information I have in this direction is embodied in a letter sent to our London office some months ago, where I made a return of the number reported as killed for the year ended (I think) December 1911. The exact figures I do not remember, but I believe the total was either 695 or 795 lions. Doubtless reference to our London people will place you in possession of the exact data.

" *Largest Bag by One Individual.*—Undoubtedly Mr. P. J. Rainey, who was credited, when I last heard, with having accounted for 120. As you are doubtless aware, he used hounds for the purpose, and the total includes, I believe, all lions run by his pack, whether shot by Rainey or his friends. Lord Delamere still, I fancy, leads with a total of 53 to his own gun. I do not quote professional hunters, as it is impossible to draw the line between those shot personally and those killed by the hunter in company with a client.

" *Mob of 46 Lions.*—Mr. H. R. M'Clure of the Government Service is, I believe, responsible for this story. The total I heard was 43, and knowing M'Clure, I feel confident the story is reliable, but I am *not* sure that it was M'Clure who saw them. The most I have ever seen consisted of mobs of 12, 11, and 10 respectively, but I have many times seen 9 and 10. The late Mr. H. A. F. Currie is said to have shot a lion out of a mob of 18.

"*Melanism and Albinism.*—No, not to my knowledge. The light or dark-maned lion is, I think, the equivalent of a blonde or brunette human.

"*Largest Number of Cubs.*—I have had very little experience here, and can only vouch for 3. Kermit Roosevelt and I shot 5 lions out of 11; of which 4 were adult (1 male and 3 females) and 7 cubs of more or less the same size, but I am not prepared to say whether these 7 cubs were all one litter. They had all been weaned—I mean that, so far as I remember, none of the females killed were in milk.

"*Habits.*—An excellent study can be obtained by entering the bulrush reed bed at Mile 300 on the Uganda Railway. I found there a quite considerable area of bulrush in the centre of the swamp, all flattened down into couches. This was evidently done to cover up the mud and water (there about 6 inches deep), and the place gives evidence of long residence of large numbers of lions. On all sides are bones and skulls (several human skulls amongst them), and I found a good number of balls of hair, each about the size of a small cricket ball. Many of these were composed of (apparently) lion hair, and I can only assume that the animals collected the hair on their spiky tongues when licking themselves. The major portion, however, appeared to be the usual hair-ball which the natives say the lion vomits after digestion, and were composed of the hair of antelope, etc.

"Although I have found lions or signs of them round and about the reed beds, my own opinion is that, where they are undisturbed, they prefer to lie up in open country, preferably on some rocky kopje commanding a wide view, and that they only take to the reeds for protection or to breed. I have certainly found more lions on the open plains, after the style of the Athi and Kapiti Plains, than anywhere else, and I daresay your own wider experience will travel thus far with my opinion.

"Regarding their food, I rather think that 'all is fish,' etc., for although the majority of kills appears to be either zebra or kongoni, these are, after all, the most common prey available. Where other animals are plentiful, the kills appear to vary more, and on one *safari* I came across a large number of wart-hog kills in some hills where lion abounded, but game other than warthog and waterbuck were scarce. I imagine that for some reason reedbuck are not popular as food for lions, as I have frequently found these animals lying up in the same swamp with *Felis leo*—particularly on the Uasin Gishu.

"Anent the much-disputed point as to which is the fiercer, lion or lioness, my own experience tends to the opinion that the lion is more apt to charge. While I have several times wounded lionesses accompanied by their cubs, without provoking a charge, I have always found that a solitary old male was a short-tempered beast, and on one occasion on the Uasin Gishu a very old male charged violently before a shot had been fired. He ran from us some 200 yards off, and by the time we had got on our ponies was out of sight, going strong through scattered timber. We missed his direction and cantered past him, when he suddenly charged us from behind, to his own undoing. I have kept no records, but, as far as I can remember, out of some twenty charges all but four or five have been lions, not lionesses. I am strongly of the opinion that the same difference in temper exists among lions as in human beings, and that there are both bold and cowardly animals. Also that, in most cases, where a lion thinks he can get away he will do so, and that he generally charges because he is unable to see his way to safety otherwise. But I will make one observation with which I feel confident you will find yourself in agreement, *i.e.*, that the only invariable rule in regard to the habits and behaviour of the lion is— that there is no invariable rule."

NOTE BY THE AUTHOR

Far more lions are killed in British East Africa than appear on the Government Returns, as sportsmen and settlers are not required, to make any return of them. According to the official " Return of Game killed in the East African Protectorate, 1911–12," there were only included on the list 76 lions and 43 lionesses, but the Game Warden adds the following remarks :—

" Lions, leopards, and cheetahs, not being included in the game list, are not always shown by sportsmen and residents on their game registers of game killed, and it is therefore impossible to make an absolutely correct return.

" The number of lions and lionesses actually shown on the game registers for the two years 1910–11 and 1911–12 totals 266. Besides this, from inquiries made, records have been obtained of 648 lions and lionesses killed during the above two years, and which have not been shown on the game registers. This makes a grand total of 914, and there is little doubt that this figure, though a large one, is below the actual number shot, trapped, and poisoned."

Personally I consider the figure 914 very much within the actual number. When persons descend to poison they keep the shameful deed, as a rule, to themselves. I have known a man poison a freshly killed zebra, and in the morning find eleven adult lions, besides innumerable vultures, hyænas, and jackals, lying dead beside the carcass. Cases have occurred where numbers of natives have been poisoned, through taking meat from poisoned bait.